HISTORY

OF THE

Second Mass. Regiment of Infantry:

SECOND PAPER.

DELIVERED BY

GEORGE H. GORDON,

MAJOR-GENERAL OF VOLUNTEERS AND COLONEL SECOND MASS. REGIMENT OF INFANTRY IN THE LATE WAR,

AT THE

ANNUAL MEETING OF THE SECOND MASS. INFANTRY ASSOCIATION, ON MAY 11, 1874.

BOSTON:
ALFRED MUDGE & SON, PRINTERS, 34 SCHOOL STREET.
1874.

HISTORY

OF THE

Second Mass. Regiment of Infantry:

SECOND PAPER.

DELIVERED BY

GEORGE H. GORDON,

MAJOR-GENERAL OF VOLUNTEERS AND COLONEL SECOND MASS. REGIMENT OF
INFANTRY IN THE LATE WAR,

AT THE

ANNUAL MEETING OF THE SECOND MASS. INFANTRY
ASSOCIATION, ON MAY 11, 1874.

BOSTON:
ALFRED MUDGE & SON, PRINTERS, 34 SCHOOL STREET.
1874.

THE ADDRESS.

CHAPTER II.

AT the earnest request of the Association, I have prepared a second paper upon the history of our regiment. My narrative is resumed with the news of our defeat at Manassas. I shall tell of the part taken by us from the hour when Gen. McClellan began the creation of the Army of the Potomac until we marched with him as part of that army for the second invasion of Virginia. I shall touch briefly upon the trials which resulted in the creation of a well-disciplined army, only hinting at the magnitude of the task to which Gen. McClellan devoted himself with a soldier's experience and a magnetic power. It will remain for the coming historian to declare that in this creation the genius of the pupil confronted the skill of the master at Appomattox, when Lee surrendered his whole army to that Army of the Potomac which grew steadily and sturdily from the seed planted by George B. McClellan.

While we were occupying Harper's Ferry as a temporary garrison, our regiment furnishing the necessary guards and its colonel commanding the fort, a daily paper received on the 25th day of July announced that the President of the United States had raised Mr. N. P. Banks, late of Massachusetts, from a private citizen to the rank of a Major-General of Volunteers, and had ordered him to relieve Gen. Patterson of his command. As a Massachusetts man, I was appealed to: What did I think of the truth of this report? "It has no foundation," I replied. "I have," I added, "a slight acquaintance with Mr. Banks, — Governor Banks, as we call him, — and I think I can assure you that he has too much good sense and good judgment to assume the responsibilities of such rank until he has fitted himself in subordinate situations to know something of a soldier's profession, — in which," I was about to add, " he is now totally inexperienced," when a knock at the door of Gen. Patterson's headquarters, where we were in discussion, announced a messenger, who brought, with the compliments of Gen. Banks to Gen. Patterson, the further information that in a few moments the former would present himself in person, to receive upon his shoulders the heavy burdens which were afterwards to be laid upon the Army of the Shenandoah.

Thus it was that the reign of Patterson within the Department of Pennsylvania was transferred to Banks, who changed the designation of the department to that of the Shenandoah. It was only one week later that the Army of the Shenandoah — with the exception of our regiment — was ordered to cross the Potomac, to take up positions in Maryland. We were left to garrison Harper's Ferry, our numbers increased by twenty cavalry-men under command of a non-commissioned officer. The order directing me to hold the outpost of Harper's Ferry was dated the 28th of July, but it was followed by another, dated the 29th of July, issued from Sandy Hook, in which three companies of the Second Massachusetts Regiment, with the cavalry detachment, were ordered to remain as a garrison at Harper's Ferry, while the remaining companies, with three guns of the Rhode Island Battery, to be commanded by the colonel of the Second Massachusetts Regiment, were ordered to cross the river into Maryland, and take position on the western face of the Maryland Heights.

Transferred to the plateau overlooking the Potomac, from an elevation half-way up the mountain, seven companies of our regiment were in position to cover the three commanded by Lieut.-Col. Andrews at Harper's Ferry. We were in an exposed location. Deprived of our tents, we sought shelter under leaves and branches. The scene was picturesque so long as the leaves were green, and the repose was sweet so long as the sticks interwoven with branches remained pliant.

In furnishing guards from Sandy Hook to Harper's Ferry; in closely watching the mounted scouts of the enemy, who occupied the hills beyond Bolivar Heights as soon as our troops were withdrawn; in drilling and in military exercises, — the poetry of life began to harden into prose; the men began to grumble.

There was no longer the excitement of a campaign, to end in victory and peace, and ensure our return to homes with the green laurels of the victor purchased at an easy price, but there was to be moulded the slow and sure conviction that the war had just begun; that home was in the distant and uncertain future; that the way now entered upon was to be trodden with a spirit and a purpose, in the upholding of which, the head was much oftener to be called into counsel than the heart. In short, on these Maryland Heights we found that the gay sport of an hour had been turned into the grim duty of a life, to be performed with all the resolve of the mind, with all the purposes of the heart, and with a sacrifice of those cherished hopes which too many indulged in when we marched gayly for the seat of war, — hopes expressed to me by one good woman, who said, looking into my face as the full companies of the Second were marching out of Camp Andrew on our last morning there, "We look to you, Col. Gordon, that you return again in safety all these young men to their homes."

Never were there soldiers who so easily braced themselves to the change. The three months' volunteers were now returning to their homes. This was, to our men, a hard sight to bear. At first some of them reproached themselves that they had enlisted for the war, then, reasoning with each other, asked eagerly if indeed they had. After much questioning, many forced themselves to the conclusion that they had not; and then, as if to strengthen conviction, they sang, in a dirge-like wail, "We are going home." None who heard will ever forget those mournful sounds as they rose evening after evening, when the lamps shone dim through the huts on the Maryland

Heights. In vain the singers tried to make themselves believe that what they sung was to come to pass ; there was no heart in the voice, no hope in the heart, and there was despair in the tones. It required but the mildest of reproof, and the briefest allusion to the history of the enlistment of our regiment, to dispel forever any further claim on the part of any member of the Second Massachusetts Regiment to be considered a three months' volunteer.

That hard work is the best cure for melancholy minds is a common experience, in which those who attended daily drills under my command will concur. I gave the men no time to brood over sorrows, and soon had the satisfaction of seeing the regiment as gay and contented as soldiers ever are ; for it is to be remembered that the temptation to grumble when there is anybody to grumble at, strong in citizens, is irresistible in those who cannot depend upon themselves, but must rely upon the watchfulness of their officers. Our men gave way to this temptation in letters to their friends, through whom by mail I received most anxious appeals, — generally, however, touching the stomach.

Says one, dated the 8th August, 1861, after alluding to the "patriotic and intelligent constituency" that the company he refers to can boast, — "The prayers of this Christian community, both private and public, have followed you." "We are not ignorant," he continues, "of the fact that many hardships and privations are incident to a soldier's life, both in the camp and field, but were not prepared to hear that some of your command have suffered much for the want of food. We had supposed the communication with Baltimore and Washington was open, that the Government had supplies, and that the quartermaster was *honest;* and we can hardly believe that it has not been the result of accident or necessity. Some have purposely disguised their feelings from their friends as long as possible, and none would wish to make their complaints public. They say they are willing to submit to *strict discipline*, to fight, and die if need be, but they can't *starve*, and not complain, when the Government is able to feed them. They all speak in the highest terms of *yourself*, and generally of their company officers. They say, however, that some of the officers in the regiment *swear* at the *men* in giving their orders; use harsh, insulting, and abusive language; and while they have seen men punished severely for tasting liquor given to them, or taking a single glass from over the fence, some of the officers are too drunk to 'perform their duty.' We have heard, in confirmation of the above, that while some of the retiring regiments *cheered* the men of the Second Regiment they *groaned* for the officers. It may not be true. These things distress our people much, and I have been almost constantly besought by those whose friends are in the regiment, to write you in relation to them." The writer closes with an admission that civilians understand but little about military affairs, and should be very careful not to interfere too much, but excuses himself because he has written "at the request of wives and mothers deeply feeling for their husbands and sons."

I have given you a picture of the returning regiments who groaned at our officers in my last paper, in which I set forth such a divergence of opinion as to the conduct and government of a regiment, that I thought it but natural my course should have displeased the Pennsylvania volunteers for three months; who, when they groaned, were absolutely marching to their homes with the sound of the enemy's guns in their ears, — turning their faces homeward against the entreaties and supplications of their commander, Gen. Patterson, that they would remain and strike one blow to prevent, if possible, the junction of Johnstone with Beauregard at Manassas; but in vain: their time was out, home they would go, and home they went, on their way groaning at the officers of this regiment in their disapprobation. It is needless to say that for any real cause, all the complaints in the letter were as little worthy attention as this.

There was also a letter from a Massachusetts Senator in Congress, dated August 12, saying: "Many of your men are writing home letters stating they are suffering for food, and these letters are having great influence. Can't this be righted?" If this honorable Senator had been more of a soldier and less of a politician, he would not have asked such foolish questions. He would have known that irregularity in the supply of food is an inevitable accompaniment of the movement of armies, and that the better the soldier the less he grumbles at the inevitable.

But the change in our circumstances from the offensive in Virginia to the defensive in Maryland wrought another change, which our enemies appreciated. The neighbors of that farmer who was paid for green grass and down-trodden fields at our first encampment at Martinsburg, had themselves suffered from an appropriation of the contents of well-stocked larders at their homes. Inspired, therefore, by the success of the Martinsburg farmer, and forgetting that the result of Manassas effectually dispelled the tender and half-regretful emotions with which we had drawn the sword, they made complaints and asked compensation for their losses. A Virginian informed me by letter that, though his ancestors came from a line of warriors, even tracing them to one of the generals of the time of Canute, the line in later days had tended rather to peaceful clergymen than to fighting men: and thus accounting for the reason why the descendant of a line of kings stoops to sue where he ought to strike; makes piteous wail over losses of butter, cream, vegetables, and ham, over clover and wheat and knocked-down shocks, and pickets in his fields; his clover-seed bags were slit with bayonets, their contents spilled. "I make no charge," says the writer, "for the provisions eaten by the men, for I have never been in the habit of charging the wayfarer; but I do complain," he adds, "that twenty-four dollars and fifty cents worth of clothing was taken from my servant man Peter"; then there follows as an outpouring of grief, an ejaculation, "None but Wisconsins would steal from the poor blacks." It was hardly politic to term us gentle tourists or needy wayfarers, or to intimate that Wisconsins would steal; and perhaps that is the reason why the complainant was not paid. Another sufferer tried it by endeavoring to fix a personal responsibility upon me, but this was in Maryland, at Sandy Hook. "Col. Gordon, Dr." the bill read. The items varied, but there was a monotonous sound of ham, jelly, and pickles; then there was an item for smashing a lock on a closet door; then something for damages to furniture and house. Whoever had the pickles had the spree: the Colonel of the Second Regiment had neither.

From the 30th of July to the 17th of August — now melted by fierce heat, and now drenched with rain that poured at night in streams from that unmitigated blessing, a rubber blanket; with men and sometimes officers, to-day impatient, grumbling, and capricious; to-morrow docile, earnest, and contented — time passed in the gradual acceptance of a discipline which not only controlled the habits but exercised an influence even over the thoughts.

By the 17th of August the alarm and excitement from an anticipated forward movement of the enemy was on the increase. Large numbers of troops at and in the immediate vicinity of Washington, to some implied a caution arising from knowledge of offensive movements in contemplation, to others not so much a knowledge as a conviction of what ought to be the movement of our enemy; and hence the military propriety of preparing to check what an enemy ought to attempt.

More than the real result to us, I think, thoughtful men feared for complications in our European relations. The results of the battle of Manassas were magnified for the transatlantic public, while lies of immense proportions were set afloat by our Northern and Southern foes, becoming huge on the regular steamer day. Thus before we left our drenched huts on the hill-side, rumors filled the air that Siegel's entire command had laid down their arms in Missouri. It was rumored in New York that 1,700 of Gen. Banks' command had been captured in Northern Virginia, and that Gen. Rosecrans was surrounded at Cumberland Gap. These were lies, as I have said; but there were some uncomfortable truths to be told, such as that recruiting was going on slowly, that dissatisfaction with the present state of things could not be dissipated but by a military success. Kentucky declaring for the Union after the battle of Manassas was the only bright spot in a very dark horizon.

Sensibly, then, we had begun to feel that the victorious armies under Lee would cross the Potomac somewhere from Washington to Williamsport. The Northern people generally feared the former, despite fortifications on the Virginia side of the Potomac, and a single bridge of about a mile in length. The guards of the Potomac knew better: the crossing would be where there were the fewest obstacles and the least opposition; and then, look out for Washington.

On the 17th of August we were withdrawn from the western slope of the Heights, and though at first the order for withdrawal directed me with our regiment to report to Col. George H. Thomas, Second Cavalry, commanding First Brigade, who was then preparing to move with most of Gen. Banks' command for the protection of Washington, a new order, dated the 17th, from the General Commanding, informed me that the "General has determined to leave your regiment in this vicinity for a few days longer," and that I would take up a position best calculated to protect the ford and not expose the main body of my regiment, and that it would be unnecessary to report to Col. Thomas as requested last evening. Our new position was designated on the 18th as at Sandy Hook. Here once more with our tents we were located upon an elevation at the foot of the eastern slope of the hill, concealed from the view of the enemy and guarding the line of the river from Harper's Ferry to Sandy Hook, a distance of five eighths of a mile.

The order designating our duty further detailed commanders and troops to guard the Potomac from Williamsport on the north to the mouth of the Monocacy on the south. Hyattstown, about twenty-six miles from Washington, was to be the headquarters of Gen. Banks.

On the 17th, also, Lt.-Col. Andrews was ordered to recross the river, bringing with him his whole force and all the flour contained in Mr. Herr's most excellent mills. Seven hundred barrels of superfine flour were transferred to our side and sent to Washington, a large part of 25,000 bushels of wheat and about 15,000 of feed used for horses destroyed.

Thus the troops in the Department of the Shenandoah entered upon their important duties. The morning of the 17th of August found us sole occupants of the hills and valleys that had so recently resounded with echoes of a multitude. Where, from many a hill-side, mountain-top, or valley, innumerable camp-fires had tendered their ruddy cheer, now but a single spot remained covered with tents. The solitude was almost desolation in its contrast.

On the 19th of August our ears were for the first time in our regimental life saluted with hostile shots. It was our first engagement, and was with a body of rebel cavalry, reported as numbering some three or four hundred, accompanied by infantry, who had entered Harper's Ferry in time to see their seven hundred barrels of superfine flour about starting along the Chesapeake and Ohio Canal for Washington city. We had a lively time for half an hour firing across the Potomac, as return compliments to the salutations of our enemy; and though none of our number were killed, and none that I ever heard of were wounded, we enjoyed the usual rewards accompanying such excitements, such as many laughable incidents, and an unshaken confidence that we had knocked two immortal souls into a better world. It was all about the flour, of course; but that did not excuse one of our most corpulent young lieutenants for exposing his very large person upon both sides of a very small sapling, which circumstance gave us much to laugh at. But at night the appearance was more threatening. For the past two or three days our sentinels, posted on the precipitate ridges of the Heights along the canal, through the tumble-down, slip-shod old town of Sandy Hook, had reported that signs of the enemy had been multiplying, that tents, wagons, and camp-fires, with now and then bodies of soldiers, had been seen; and these reports gave day by day increased numbers.

Upon these indications of the proximity of the enemy, I made the best disposition I could to repel any attempt to cross the river by ford or ferry, or to annoy us from the other side. The distance across the river where our pontoon bridge had been located was less than one sixth of a mile, — not a comfortable distance with long-ranged rifles that kill at a mile and a quarter. Two companies, well concealed, covered the ford, with a practicable road at their backs across the mountain, — a road built by Capt. Underwood, of Co. I, to save exposure from the fire that an enemy could deliver from the commanding eminence upon the Shenandoah side, — deliver plumply down upon the tow-path of the canal or the track of the railway, where the only possible passage had been chiselled out of the side of the mountain. It was late at night on the 19th day of August that I lay down on a bundle of straw and single blanket to sleep; but I had hardly lost myself when the officer of the guard ushered a stranger into my tent, bearing the following dispatch, which I read by the light of the officer's lantern: —

"COL. GORDON, — I am directed by Col. Donnelly to send a messenger to you with information that the rebels are marching on Harper's Ferry 6,000 strong.
"Yours very respectfully,
"E. F. BROWN,
"Lieut.-Col. Twenty-Eighth Regt. N. Y. V.
"BERLIN, MD., August 19, 1861."

I put a few hasty questions to the messenger, who apologized for his haste, as he must hurry back to his regiment, though he believed the dispatch to me to be well founded, from recent signs and movements. I remained for a moment alone, looking down from the little eminence partially surrounded with trees, where my tent stood, upon the thousand sleepers in their tents, so still and quiet that the rushing waters of the Potomac were audible. The indistinct light of the moon revealed the dark sides of the Blue Ridge swelling into most gigantic proportions on the Shenandoah shore. The murmur of the katydids, mingling with the sweet and solemn voices that break on the ear in the deep hush of midnight, and the silent camp, so picturesque on the hill-side, whispered of peace and tranquillity; and yet behind those hills, pressing on to our unprotected front, were at least 6,000 to our 1,000. I had not a single piece of artillery to oppose the many which they could bring to cover the ford. With Gen. Banks' column had departed the three pieces that had threatened Harper's Ferry from the other side of the Heights.

To me, and according to my best judgment, the attempt of the enemy to cross the river in my front was probable. It was more likely to succeed than if attempted at Washington (which was greatly feared by military and unmilitary minds). It would have been in entire accord with all military principles governing the crossing of rivers defended by an enemy; for it would have been at a practicable ford, the nearest to an objective point, — the city of Washington, — and to reach a country in which true sympathy would have been found. That it was practicable to scale and take these Heights, in the face of a good defence, Stonewall Jackson proved one year later, before we attacked Lee at Antietam; and whether wise or otherwise, that some commanders do cross rivers at night, rivers too that are not fordable, without any consideration of how they are to get back again, provided all things do not turn out as it is expected and a larger force is encountered than is looked for, or they are not supported as they fancy they ought to be, we had abundant and melancholy evidence some few weeks later at

Ball's Bluff, on the Potomac. That this attack was to be met, and that I had neither the guns nor the numbers to meet it successfully, was my conviction, not less earnest than my determination to send for artillery and reinforcements, and to get them, if possible, in season to fight with a show of success. To give my whole command all the rest I could, I did not call a groom, but saddling my horse myself, mounted, and rode hastily into that pestilential hole of Sandy Hook, to the telegraph office in the hotel. Buried in profound slumber, it was some minutes before I could arouse the operator, and more before I could make the stupid warders at the gates of sense convey the least intelligence to the brain. Once, however, at his instrument, I watched with anxiety for a signal; the welcome click replied. The wires were not cut, were intact, though they skirted the banks of the Potomac for a distance of almost twelve miles to the Point of Rocks before turning easterly to Frederick.

Thank God for the wires I devoutly did, for upon them depended my relief.

"Where shall I telegraph?" asks the operator.

"To headquarters."

Rapidly sounds the instrument, as in vain we call for a reply.

"What's the matter?" I ask.

"Am afraid there's no night operator," he says.

"Continue your call; don't cease," I urge with impatience.

Rattling away at the instrument resounding through that dimly lighted room, and waiting with anxiety, while minutes, precious minutes, were passing, for some friendly greeting from the outer darkness, a quarter of an hour passes, and no answer yet

"Try some other place," I quickly order.

"Where, sir?" asks the operator.

"Where? Some place where we have troops and artillery," I answer. "Try Frederick."

Again sounds that monotonous rattle, and again in vain; no answer.

"Keep on," I say; and again no answer.

"What can you do?" I urge.

"I might try Baltimore," he suggests; "perhaps some one is awake there."

"Well, try Baltimore then."

"Is this a failure too?" I ask, as nothing comes from that infernal instrument but that monotonous click, which, to my undisciplined ear, varied not in sound.

"Try some other station in Baltimore then." And again that devilish ditty, that galop of the echoes of resounding metal. For a few moments it was the same straining vision, and the same painful watching for a sound, to be relieved at last by the welcome hail, away off in Baltimore, ninety miles away, at some distant railroad station.

"What do you want?" asks this blessed imp of lightning as he rides through the darkness on a flash of electricity.

"Is there a night operator within twenty miles of me?" I demand.

"Yes, at Frederick," he responds.

"Who is there at Frederick?" I ask.

"Troops, and Gen. Fitz John Porter," is the reply.

My fingers ache in sympathy with the late effort of my luckless operator to arouse a sentiment of life in Frederick, but I try, and at last comes the splutter of this indolent genius, who certainly did not claim to be the servant of any lamp or ring in my possession, as he cried out, —

"What do you want?"

"Who is there of our army at Frederick? is what I want."

"Gen. Porter," comes to me from the wires.

It was the work of a moment to ask where he was, and to learn that he was sleeping at the hotel; and then to direct that he be immediately informed that I was awaiting at the end of the wire an answer to this dispatch: "The enemy, numbering 6,000, are marching upon Harper's Ferry. I am here with my regiment, but no artillery. If the enemy has artillery I cannot hold the place. What shall be done? Answer quickly."

"I will carry him this dispatch and answer in twenty minutes," replies the operator. It was one o'clock in the morning of the 20th of August, — not time enough to make great preparation to meet this coming force, whose tramp I could almost hear, I fancied, on the shores of the Potomac. I was somewhat nervous, I admit; events of the past few weeks had made me so. As patiently as I could, I counted ten of the twenty minutes as they passed off into eternity, then twenty and thirty, but no reply. "Ask for an answer."

No response for a moment, and then the cool reply, "I have important dispatches to Baltimore, and cannot leave to carry your message." To say that I was as mild as a morning-glory would be a metaphor, but not a true one.

Cannot leave in this important moment, at a time when so much may depend upon my dispatch; Frederick twenty miles away; impossible to send from here; the hours passing swiftly on, and no increase to my force! "Tell him he must go," I replied.

"I cannot," replies the operator; "he has cut off all communication with this place, and will not get my dispatch."

"Can you jump him," I ask, "to a place beyond?"

"Yes, I can reach Baltimore again."

"Do so, and tell the operator there to tell the operator at Frederick that he must deliver my message immediately."

The faithful slave of the telegraph at Baltimore so promptly stirred up that ugly genius of Frederick that in a moment he answered, "Now I will go"; and soon returned with the sleepy message from Gen. Porter, that Col. Gordon has his orders.

Tell him to come down to the telegraph office and talk with me," I hurl out into the night on the wings of the lightning; and in a few moments the wires speak, — "Here he comes."

Then, looking intently into each other's faces though more than twenty miles away, we spoke with tongues of fire. I told him of the three hundred cavalry and infantry, and scouts seen around Harper's Ferry, then of the warning dispatch of the six thousand received here an hour since, and that I thought it more than probable I should be attacked at daylight.

"Well," says Porter, "Gen. Banks' instructions are, to dispute the passage of fords, and if too strongly pressed, to retire slowly towards, in this case, Buckeyestown. Col. Donnelly has two pieces of artillery, which he is directed to send to you if required. Call on Col. Geary to send you two by express train. Can the enemy ford the river? I suggest you send your baggage to the rear; daylight will show the enemy not so strong as represented. Send a messenger to Col. Leonard, to withdraw towards Boonsboro' and Buckeyestown, and send your baggage there; but don't retire entirely without making your enemy feel you; he will not follow or attack a determined front."

Thus ended our colloquy. It was two o'clock in the morning as I bade Gen. Porter good-night, mounted my horse, and returned to camp. Cautiously I aroused the field officers and communicated to them my dispatches; then the men were awakened, tents struck, horses harnessed, wagons packed, fires lighted, and rations cooked.

Dispatches were sent in various directions; down the river to Col. Donnelly of the Twenty-Eighth N. Y., for artillery,— a message carried by Dr. Sargent, who pressingly urged himself as a volunteer for a ride of ten miles. In reply, Dr. Sargent brought a reply from the Lieut.-Col. Brown who had reported the approach of the enemy, that Lieut.-Col. Tompkins of the Rhode Island Battery would be sent me, and although this would leave them destitute, they would take the chances, etc. This dispatch, a curious mixture of ignorance and bravado, well illustrated the offspring that newspaper clamor and editor generals gave birth to in the earlier stages of our war. Pert in proportion to their ignorance, mistaking an assumed indifference to precautions for real valor, this class failed in all the essentials for military success, and were deserted even by their impudence in times of trial.

I also dispatched a messenger to Sharpsburg to Col. Leonard, acquainting him with the orders received through Col. Porter for his withdrawal towards Boonsboro' and Buckeyestown, and, further informing him of the dispatches about the enemy, asked him to move in my direction that he might aid me if necessary; to which, long after daylight next morning, I received a reply from Col. Leonard, that he understood it would be out of his way, in withdrawing towards Boonsboro' and Buckeyestown, to come around by Maryland Heights, and therefore plainly implied that he would not come.

I also sent a dispatch to Col. Geary, at Point of Rocks, informing him of the reported movement of the enemy, and that from the entry of a heavy force of rebel cavalry and some infantry into the town of Harper's Ferry, I thought there was no doubt truth in Lieut.-Col. Brown's dispatch, and asking him for two pieces of artillery, for which I would send a train of cars if he would return the same with ammunition and artillerists.

Then having taken all the precautions I could for a proper defence if attacked, I threw myself exhausted upon a bundle of straw, and fell into a quiet slumber. As the first faint blushes of morning showed themselves in the east, I was aroused, and prepared for an engagement. Daylight invading the domain of night first brought mountain, trees, and camp into more distinct view, then touched them with that pallid hue, so often to be seen thereafter, so well remembered as the beginning of many days in which, before the merciful night closed in, we had supped full of many horrors. Then came the sun, the glorious, beaming, hopeful sun, slowly rising, and touching with his golden color the mountain-top, lighting up the gorges, and driving with his smiles of peace the darker spirits of the night away.

But still no sound of the expected fray, no reports from our watchful sentinels, when lo! from the summit of the Heights, there all quiet in her morning dreams lay Harper's Ferry, as much unconscious of the 6,000 strong reported by that Lieut.-Col. Brown as if this force had never any other existence than in his too excited brain, from whence, in short, they may have been conjured up, for there, and there alone, were they ever discovered. To say that I was disgusted, angry, and mortified is to draw it mildly ; and to say, here and now, that I became reconciled only when I made up my mind that it was possible my preparations had deterred an enemy, if there was any, from an attack.

It was not long after sunrise when I received an order from Gen. Banks, issued the day before, directing me to join my regiment to Col. Donnelly's, the two to proceed *via* Buckeyestown to rejoin their brigades. Ours, under command of Gen. Abercrombie, we were informed, was now at Hyattstown, where the army would be for the present. Col. Thomas's brigade would reach Hyattstown probably to-morrow (the 21st), the order said. The order then continued : "The General wishes this movement to take place as soon as it possibly can be effected. Before leaving Harper's Ferry, he wishes you to bring off, if you can in a short time, and if not, to destroy the wheat and mill-stones in the mills at Harper's Ferry, provided you can do so without endangering the safety of your command." Recommending haste, though not precipitation, I was directed to bring off the telegraph instruments and destroy the wires.

This order reached me about the same hour that a telegram was handed me from Gen. Fitz John Porter, saying that the orders I had just received were to go to me last night, but hoping if I got a chance I would pitch into the enemy; that Kenly, at Williamsport, was ordered to watch the fords at Harper's Ferry, and Geary at Monocacy, and advising, if I should go into Harper's Ferry, that I should destroy the mill-stones. And there was a telegram from Col. Geary, at Point of Rocks, that he was directed not to permit cars to pass that point (which he had christened Camp Korpony) should the enemy cross, or attempt so to do, above him; followed shortly after by another dispatch from the same officer, announcing that he would relieve me to-morrow with a detachment.

During the remaining hours of the 20th I again entered Harper's Ferry, to carry final destruction to Herr's flour-mill and its contents. With the execution of this order Lieut.-Col. Andrews was charged. Crossing the Ferry with a small force, which he threw out as pickets upon landing, his operations were covered with my newly-arrived artillery and additional force upon the Heights, the canal, and railroad. How to move with the most telling rapidity in the destruction of a large mill, I believe Lt.-Col. Andrews has proved most successfully to be, in first determining the point at which the whole motive power is applied; and if this is in a well, as it usually is in mills moved by water power, first set in motion with all possible force the upright shaft, and then plunge — when at its utmost speed, well poised and swift — plunge down an iron bar among the cogs that take and impart motion to connecting wheels. So did Lt.-Col. Andrews. The crash, resounding above the roar of iron wheels, was followed by a tremor as when a giant dies from mortal thrust; and Herr's famous flour-mills were useless for the war. A large part of the wheat remaining was thrown into the Potomac, and then Lt.-Col. Andrews withdrew without molestation. It was not until the morning of the 21st of August that I was ready to leave for Buckeyestown, at which time we turned our faces towards Washington, as a better move for its protection and the defence of Maryland.

Hardly had I withdrawn my artillery from the hill and my pickets from the front, when the enemy's pickets swarmed into Harper's Ferry. Joining the Twentieth N. Y. Regiment at Berlin, we trailed across a country of unbridged streams, through which our horses and mules splashed with their burdens, and over which our men passed in file on trunks of prostrate trees. Houses were small and shaky, and not many of them; negroes were lazy and fat; and the corn-fields rejoiced in gigantic stalks. On the 23d we encamped at the foot of a steep hill, in the flourishing village of Hyattstown. We had made twenty-one miles in three days. From hill-top to valley all around us the ground was dotted with white-roofed tents and wagon-tops. It was by the light of the stars that we breakfasted on the morning of the 29th of August, and prepared to move still farther southward to concentrate for the defence of Washington.

In the afternoon of the 30th of August our regiment, at the end of its day's march, turned from the road-side into a field within the town of Darnstown. The single farm-house in view, with the grounds adjacent, called Pleasant Hill, comprised all we could discover of the village; for the clouds hung densely around us, and the earth and sky were moist with rain. We were cold, hungry, and tired. In my official capacity I ate a supper prepared for another: doubtless my rank saved me from a blessing — after the meal. That we were to move forward on the morrow I believed, — I did not know where; but somewhere, in some position, to take our part in a general attack upon the enemy. The morning came and went, and we moved not. A week passed; then a month; and but few days were left of another, and still my tent covered the same spot upon which it was pitched upon the first day of our arrival. For nearly two months, upon the hills, in the valleys, and along the highways of Darnstown, were clustered the camps of our division, with their camp-fires at night dotting the ground with flame. For almost two months we heard at evening music from various regimental bands, as it fell faintly from the distance, or swelled in harmony around, until the drum and fife, or the bugle-call, breaking forth into the tattoo, announced the hour for sleep. From day to day, and from night to night, sound and sight repeated itself, until it was not easy to hold in view the grandeur of the achievement, in the strife of the spirit, with the tedious details of the hour. Even our sentinels, watching the Potomac, six miles away from our encampment, softened their hostile glances, and swimming across the river exchanged friendly conferences and hearty hand-shakes with their rebel neighbors. That the round of duties became tedious must be admitted: provision returns for pork, beans, flour, rice, tea, coffee, et cetera, were presented with unfailing regularity; there was no break in morning reports of present and absent, of approvals and disapprovals, of attending reveilles, drills, and parades. It was at this camp that our drills began to receive almost unmerited attention.

The confusion into which our battalion seemed to be plunged during these simple movements on that bit of ground called forth great praise when we were extricated and in line again. Who will forget that double column, closed in mass, the countermarch and deploy, the changes of front forward and to the rear, all at double quick, as, with a snap, lines of battle were formed forward, to the rear, to the right, and the left; and who will say that the continually increasing happiness of our men, their contentment, a thousand-fold greater than when on Maryland Heights, was not due to the constant praise bestowed upon them for their marked drill and discipline?

While our discipline troubled one Massachusetts regiment, it excited a spirit of emulation in another. To equal the "Gordon boys" in drill and discipline was an aspiration of the Thirteenth; to interfere with our discipline was at one time the desire of the Twelfth. When and why is worth narrating: Our camps overlooked each other, and were separated by a shallow gully. Looking into our camp one morning, soon after our arrival, the officers and men of the Twelfth Massachusetts, known as the Webster Regiment, saw one of our privates tied up to a tree near the guard-house. To such punishment had he been sentenced, for some military offence, by a court-martial. He was to be tied up for three days in succession, an hour at a time each day. Hardly had this scene met the eyes of the Twelfth, when they greeted it with loud shouts of disapprobation. "Cut him down! cut him down!" they cried, as in a tumultuous body they advanced threateningly towards us. In vain did their officers try to control them. For a few moments the aspect was threatening. Our guard was promptly turned out under arms; the officers and soldiers of the Second calmly awaited the issue. There was but a single exception, — a frisky Irishman, probably belonging to Company I, leaped once or twice in the air, howling with sympathy; he was promptly knocked down by an officer, and suppressed in the guard-tent. At length expostulations prevailed where orders were useless. The officers of the Twelfth urged their men to desist, and during the remainder of the hour they were quiet.

In the afternoon Col. Webster informed me that if that man was to be tied up again in full view of his regiment, he would not be responsible for the consequences. "Yes, he could control his men," he replied, in answer to my question.

The man would be tied up in the same place, I assured him. "Then I shall take my men out to drill at that hour," he answered. This assurance on the part of Col. Webster was serious. A rush within our lines was possible. Seeing a ruse, suppose they should refuse to go to drill? It was very much like a mutiny in the division, and was quite time for the General Commanding to interfere. I laid the matter before him, in time for action before the next day's punishment. It was quite evident, I insisted, that Col. Webster could not control his men; and it was equally clear these men must be controlled. The punishment I was inflicting was by sentence of a court; was not cruel. Upon the immediate and utter extinction of any such insubordination as had been shown by the Twelfth depended whether this division should be an army or a mob.

"You are quite right, sir," replied Gen. Banks.

"Then, sir, will you order to report to me, to-morrow, at my encampment, a squadron of cavalry, and a battery, with authority to use their arms in the suppression of any mutiny that may take place near my camp?"

"I will order them," replied Gen. Banks.

I thanked him, and retired, to meet Col. Webster approaching General Banks' headquarters for an interview.

Next morning, and but a few minutes before the appointed hour for the execution of the sentence, an orderly delivered to me a note from Gen. Banks substantially as follows:—

Sir, — Since publicity is no part of the sentence of the court-martial in the case of the man to be tied up, I would suggest that the remainder of the sentence be executed in a less conspicuous place.

Instantly I directed Major Dwight to lay before Gen. Banks the result of such a concession to a mutinous demand, and to protest with all his power against any change whatever in the punishment. Major Dwight returned in a few minutes, to say that Gen. Banks, as soon as he had dispatched my note, had ridden rapidly away, leaving no word at his headquarters of his movements. It was but a brief time before the hour, — not enough to make pursuit of Gen. Banks possible. The Commanding General had shirked the responsibility. Like Halifax, once the notorious Speaker of the House of Lords in England, Gen. Banks was a most sagacious trimmer. If there was bloodshed, he had suggested a prevention; if there was no affray, he had not ordered a concession. Neither battery nor cavalry had reported, and now was the hour for the execution of sentence. Sending for the officer of the day, I ordered him to make no change in the mode of execution of the sentence; and none was made. At the appointed hour, while the sentence was being carried into effect in the same place as before, the Colonel of the Twelfth Massachusetts Regiment hastily marched his men far out of sight or sound of our camp. They returned long after the hour had expired, overcome with fatigue, but with not a trace of mental laceration through our cruelty. For the third time and last, on the third morning, the same expedient was adopted while the remainder of the sentence was executed.

Almost two hundred years ago, during the reign of the Prince of Orange, the people of England looked with apprehension upon the organization of Regulars.

Macaulay has well portrayed the dangers that threatened the country through mobs of undisciplined men calling themselves soldiers. I cannot forbear quoting him : —

"It was necessary there should be regular soldiers, and it was indispensable, both to their efficiency and to the security of every other class, that they should be kept under a strict discipline. An ill-disciplined army has ever been a more costly and a more licentious militia, impotent against a foreign enemy, and formidable only to the country which it is paid to defend. A strong line of demarcation, therefore, must be drawn between the soldiers and the rest of the community. For the sake of public freedom they must, in the midst of freedom, be placed under a despotic rule; they must be subject to a sharper penal code and to a more stringent code of procedure than are administered by the ordinary tribunals. Some acts which in the citizen are innocent, must in the soldier be crimes; some acts, which in the citizen are punished with fine or imprisonment, must in the soldier be punished with death. The machinery by which courts of law ascertain the guilt or innocence of an accused citizen is too slow and too intricate to be applied to an accused soldier. For of all the maladies incident to the body politic, military insubordination is that which requires the most prompt and drastic remedies. If the evil be not stopped as soon as it appears, it is certain to spread, and it cannot spread far without danger to the very vitals of the commonwealth. For the general safety, therefore, a summary jurisdiction of terrible extent must, in camps, be intrusted to a rude tribunal, composed of men of the sword."

If the opinions of men whose judgment is entitled to great consideration may be quoted in defence of the policy we adopted for the government of our regiment, I may refer to Macaulay's most excellent comments as vindicating our judgment, when opposed by Governor Andrew at West Roxbury, and for a second time by Governor Banks and the Twelfth Massachusetts Regiment at Darnstown.

I now resume our history, to speak first of the portentous orders of those days,—stampedes we called them,—when we moved but to halt again upon the land of some unfortunate farmer, to trample down his fields, burn his fences, eat his harvests, pluck and roast his growing corn, decapitate his geese, drink all his milk, eat all his butter and eggs, and occupy all his house and barns. Such cases were grave attacks of stampedes, but generally they were of a milder type. It was in camp at Darnstown that I was once aroused at midnight with the order, "Get your command in immediate readiness to move, but don't wake your men until further orders," upon which I proceeded to put myself in immediate readiness by pulling on my stockings, after which, overpowered with sleep, I was aroused by the bright daylight to the consciousness of another stampede.

When the advancing season brought cold nights after hot days, when the murky atmosphere of fall rested upon the hills, and the soft Indian summer began to lay hold of the landscape, there fell upon us storms, in which the strong winds swayed our tents, struggling with the flimsy fastenings. Can we ever forget the crashing of the thunder, the glare of the lightning, and the moaning of the tempest, as the big drops pelted our frail covering, and the clouds brooded over us with a deeper than Egyptian darkness,—this war of nature, with a whole army enfolded in the arms of sleep, patriot and rebel, on each side of the dividing Potomac, while the sentinels of both armies cowered beneath the storm? If ever a feeling of awe steals into the human soul, it is in the presence of elemental powers; and there, in such presence, while we were emulating the powers of nature with our engines of destruction, I could, for one, only raise my thoughts, in the midst of the storm and the power and the on-coming carnage, praying that God, great, good, and beneficent, might bear me bravely on.

It was easy in those days to arouse that spirit of obedience to the will of the Lord which, rather than adventure, leads men to deeds of noble daring. It was easier to move the cold nature of our New England men by exhortation than by allurement; they were rather Puritans than Cavaliers: and what Puritans can do when their blood is thoroughly up has been proved on many fields of battle.

It was on the 22d of September, on Sunday, that our honored friend and associate, the Rev. Dr. Lothrop, while on a visit to our camp, preached to our regiment in the front yard of the single house near our encampment at Darnstown.

The enclosure was crowded with companies of our regiment. The road beyond and the edge of the adjacent field was filled with men from the division, silent and attentive. Out of his heart the preacher spoke, as if inspired. How could he speak otherwise? There on either side of that river, where repose the ashes of the Father of his Country, there almost within sight of Mount Vernon, were the citizens of a common country gathered in arms for the attack and defence of that capital which bears the name of the immortal Washington. On that same Sunday morning, with our common glory a common inheritance there, on the other bank of the Potomac, were ministers of the Gospel casting their eyes upward to God in prayerful petition for success in what they claimed to be a cause as holy as this in which we were engaged. It was not strange that the spirit which animated our ancestors fell upon us at that hour; it was not strange that we believed ourselves a chosen people, divinely commissioned to slay the sinners on the other side of our dividing Jordan. The Stars and Stripes were invested with a sanctity that made them the ark of the covenant of the Lord,—a banner before which the waters should again roll back their flood, as they did before the high-priests of old. Under the passionate exhortation of that Sunday morning we went back to our encampment, our ears ringing with the words which God aforetime spoke to Joshua,—"Have I not commended thee? Be strong, and of good courage; be not afraid, neither be thou dismayed; for I the Lord thy God am with thee whithersoever thou goest."

On the 26th of September my command was increased by four other regiments and a Rhode Island Battery. The regiments were the Fifth Connecticut, Nineteenth and Twenty-Eighth New York, and Forty-Sixth Pennsylvania. I held this command for two weeks, but this was long enough to contrast their discipline with ours. Upon my first visit to the Forty-Sixth Pennsylvania, I found one sentinel sitting down on his post, while another, as I galloped towards him, whipped his musket across both shoulders and dashed up and down, imitating quite creditably my horse's gallop, but with such a great grin of fun and good-nature that I laughed without control. Here, too, I found, in anticipation of the coming movement no doubt, dressed in full uniform and enrolled as a soldier, regularly mustered into the service, a young woman of about eighteen years of age. She had been in the regiment about a month; until within a day or two there had been no suspicion of her sex. I am not aware that her presence tended to elevate the standard of character in her company. She could smoke a pipe, and swear like a veteran. I ordered her to be discharged, for which I may yet be denounced and politically doomed.

It was here too that (Congress having enacted that a band-leader should receive the pay and allowances of a second lieutenant of infantry) the Governor of Connecticut sent a commission of second lieutenant to the leader of Col. O. S. Ferry's regiment, the Fifth Connecticut. The colonel, appealing to me, asked what he should do. "Shall I consider the band a *quasi* company, he asks, under orders of a second lieutenant? The band-leader says, Gen. Banks tells him his office is that of second lieutenant, but his functions must be limited to the band. What becomes of the drum-major? If I am ordered to detail an officer on signal service, can I detail the band-leader? Does a band-leader become a second lieutenant because his pay is designated to be the amount received by a second lieutenant of infantry, any more than the other members of the band become sergeants and corporals of engineers, whose pay they draw?" I believe that band-leader pranced around in shoulder-straps for a time, but he was never suffered to consider himself a second lieutenant.

And it was at our camp in Darnstown that the exasperated soldier of a regiment of volunteers, tied to a wagon-tail, by order of the major of his regiment, for insubordination and drunkenness, gnawing off his thongs, with his musket shot the major dead, just as they were passing our encampment. For this act the soldier was tried by a Court, sitting on our grounds, of which Major Wilder Dwight was President.

On the 7th of October, in observance of a day of fasting and prayer which the President of the United States had suggested, the whole division moved to a field, where, formed in close columns of battalions, they stood with uncovered heads before a stand, from which, after prayers, a sermon by our chaplain was delivered. Then, accompanied by all the regimental bands, a mighty sound rolled upward in the majestic strains of Old Hundred, as with united voice the whole division sung these verses written for the occasion : —

ARMY HYMN.

AIR. — *Old Hundred.*

O LORD OF HOSTS, Almighty King !
Behold the sacrifice we bring !
To every arm Thy strength impart,
Thy Spirit shed thro' every heart.

Wake in our breasts the living fires,
The holy faith that warmed our sires.
Thy hand hath made our nation free :
To die for her is serving thee.

Be Thou a pillared flame to show
The midnight snare, the silent foe ;
And when the battle thunders loud,
Still guide us in its moving cloud.

> God of all nations, sovereign Lord!
> In Thy dread name we draw the sword;
> We lift the starry flag on high
> That fills with light our stormy sky.
>
> From treason's rent, from murder's stain,
> Guard Thou its folds till peace shall reign, —
> Till fort and field, till shore and sea
> Join our loud anthem, PRAISE TO THEE!

So long had we now been located in one spot that our camp began to grow into a tawdry kind of village: we had tradesmen with their shanties, tempting our troops with pies, cakes, and soap; daguerrean saloons, — small black boxes, covered with tarpaulins; and a marvellous structure erected by our wagon-master. It was a shelter with a roof handsomely thatched, and large enough to protect the sixty or seventy horses belonging to us, that had been shivering in the chill nights. Such preparations gave assurances of permanency; but who can tell where to-morrow a soldier will dwell?

> "Lo, there the soldier, rapid architect!
> Builds his light town of canvas, and bustles momently
> With arms and neighing steeds and mirth and quarrel.
> The motley market fills; the road, the streams
> Are crowded with new freights; trade stirs and hurries.
> But on some morrow's morn all suddenly
> The tents drop down, the horde renews its march.
> Dreary and solitary as a church-yard,
> The meadows and down-trodden seed flat lie,
> And the year's harvest is gone utterly."

On the 13th of October I relinquished command of my brigade, again assuming command of our regiment. The weather was cold, but with burrowing in the ground and blankets we were warm. While the people were crying, "On to Richmond!" the men were making ovens. In these rude affairs all kinds of cooking was performed, — meat roasted, pork and beans and bread baked, and a half-barrel of doughnuts cooked at once for a single company.

But the people were impatient. Newspaper editors were clamorous; all our Dames were Quickleys; the country was indifferent to Napoleon's maxim, "Never fight unless the advantages of victory are much greater than losses by defeat." Another defeat at Manassas might involve fatal results, so McClellan's policy was one of extreme caution. In the mean time fleets were being prepared to descend upon the Southern sea-coast, and keep some of the Southern soldiers farther south than in Virginia. And still we waited, and the still cold weather came on apace, to make us shiver o' nights, and swallow a great deal of smoke over wood-fires in front of our tents. Some of our officers grumbled because for many days they had not seen a looking-glass. It was drill, drill, drill; some reading of military books; a great deal of reading of the newspapers, a great deal of imagination, and a vast deal of hope.

There was much speculation in our camps: would the enemy cross the river? Was this delay that McClellan might strengthen his position, raise the depressed spirits of our men, and add real solidity to our army? See, said some, what made the disaster of Bull Run possible, — soldiers without drill, their time of enlistment expiring; soldiers who did not enlist to fight, but to brag; men without discipline, not caring a rush for their officers. Their blood was not aroused, for they did not believe us to be really at war with a merciless and resolved rebel force; so they walked on tiptoe where should have been a ringing tramp. Against such a condition of things, it was urged, McClellan will provide; he is fortifying himself at Washington, on the west at Alexandria, and on the north, within eighteen miles of us, at Tennallytown; he will not leave Washington defenceless.

On the 19th of October five of our friends from Boston dined with us at the headquarters' mess-table, — Messrs. Sidney Bartlett, William Amory and son, Jefferson Coolidge, and F. D'Hauteville. The dinner we gave them is, I am told, still fragrant in their memory. If I had informed our sympathizing and pitying friends at home of the four chickens happily roasted, of the tenderly-boiled leg of mutton and its rich surroundings of butter sauce, of the sweet and Irish potatoes, of the tomatoes, Indian pudding, and whiskey and water that made up the fare of the suffering soldier in the field, I fear the "New York Tribune" would have howled "Onward to Richmond!" with more relentless energy than ever before.

At this date, too, a rumor reached us that there had been a fight at Harper's Ferry, with a report that a Col. Ashby, as prisoner, had just passed through our camp to headquarters. Nine days before, our Capt. Tompkins, commanding the Rhode Island Battery at Sandy Hook, had written me that there were fourteen hundred rebels at Halltown with two twelve-pounders, and that a Major Gould wished him to take his guns over to-day. "As the river is very high," writes the captain, "should we, under such circumstances, be obliged to retreat, we shall have a rough time of it." This was about all there was to the whole rumor. The captain had more wisdom than the major. Had it been otherwise, the lesson of crossing an unfordable stream to attack a superior force, relying upon artillery, with no bridge or preparation to return in case of defeat, — this lesson might have saved us that experience which, coming from a similar attempt at Ball's Bluff eleven days later, filled the country with horror.

If they served no other purpose, these rumors made our officers groan with impatience. They grumbled because *they* were to have no chances, and finally, impatience bursting the bonds of reason, they initiated the movement which afterwards resulted in a petition to the General Government to be permitted to fight something, somewhere or somehow. This ardent zeal, born of inexperience, was simply the outburst of high-toned men, who, having come from their homes to accomplish something as soldiers, were much afraid the war would end and none of the Second Massachusetts be able to shoulder his crutch and show how fields were won. Alas for

Winchester and Cedar Mountain, Antietam and Gettysburg! While we may exclaim, "O blindness, to the future kindly given," we may, we do rest assured that if even there any true prophet had lifted the veil and pointed to the shadows of coming events, Mudge would still have rung out, as he threw himself at the head of his regiment, to die at Gettysburg, "Forward the Second! It is murder, but it is an order." Dwight would still have traced with fainting hand, as his life-blood was wasting away at Antietam, "I think I die in victory." Shaw would still have moved forward, though before him had opened the path which, later, led to his noble death on the parapet of Wagner. Savage, Abbott, and Cary; Williams, Goodwin, and Perkins, would not have faltered if before them had been mirrored their own silent forms clasped in the cold embrace of death on the field of Cedar Mountain; nor would the rank and file that made so rich the history of the Second, with their sublime courage, on many historic fields,—nor would they have put the cup away from their lips, but would have drunk it even to the very dregs.

It was on the 21st day of October that an order, issuing from Gen. Banks, to hold ourselves in readiness, with five days' rations, cooked and uncooked, and to report for orders to Brigadier-Gen. Hamilton, commanding Second Brigade, was followed within a short time by a note from that officer to move at once without baggage, leaving a guard to come on with tents, baggage, rations, etc. "You will take the lead; the other regiments will follow. Wait for me at Poolsville," was the hasty ending. At the same time a private note from Major Copeland thought I "would like to know that Gen. Stone and his army were at Leesburg, with very little fighting."

It was nine o'clock at night that we turned hurriedly from the warmth of the huge fires that were devouring the superfluous fixtures of our late residence, to file out from the ruddy glare into darkness, and take the road to Poolsville, distant about eight miles. Our course was westerly and towards the most distant point in the abrupt bend of the Potomac at Conrad's Ferry. Until we reached Poolsville, which was one o'clock in the morning of the 22d, I had no definite idea of the purpose of our march. That Gen. Stone had crossed into Virginia, and that we were to follow and sustain or co-operate, was my belief; but now came the first droppings of disaster: dark figures standing by the road-side muttered, as we passed, about entire defeat in a fight that had lasted all day; then came rumors of the death of Col. Baker, commanding, and the report that his body was lying in the house, just discernible in the darkness, by which our column was passing; then followed, — " Driven back across the river; the Twentieth Regiment, Col. Lee, and the Fifteenth Regiment, Col. Devens, entirely cut up," etc. etc. Paying but little heed to this not exhilarating information, I pushed on a few miles farther, to encounter more positive evidence of disaster, — men half naked, hatless, shoeless, hastening in the pouring rain towards Poolsville, exclaiming as they rushed by, " We are defeated with immense loss; our regiment is cut to pieces; Col. Lee is a prisoner, Col. somebody killed, and Col. somebody else trying to hide away in a hay-stack." Then came indignant protests: " They outnumbered us ten to one. Shame to put us in such a position!" Then came strong adjectives condemning souls to nameless places. Then more, recitative, " We had to take to the water and swim, and they shot us while swimming; many men are drowned. We got the best of them the first part of the day, but they received reinforcements in large numbers, and we could n't. Col. Devens told us to save ourselves; took off his boots, said 'I'm going to swim for it, boys. I've done all I can for you,' and he escaped."

As we pushed forward, the crowd of disorganized and shivering fugitives that trailed to the rear became greater. Occasionally there were plucky exclamations, and congratulations that our column was passing, " And if we had only had them fellers an hour or two ago, we would have thrashed them." As daylight began to break through the heavy clouds, we came to the river at Conrad's Ferry, a little less than four miles from Poolsville. Three motionless forms, wrapped in blankets, were being buried by their comrades, as we halted by their graves. Wearied with fatigue and shivering with cold, unsheltered from the pitiless rain that continued to fall in torrents, we saw the wretched daylight break upon a closing scene over which the elements themselves seemed to brood in sympathy. Our march had ended, and now from many living witnesses the stories of the fugitives were corroborated.

The circumstances that gave rise to the battle of Ball's Bluff, and the main features of that massacre, belong to this story, and may be told in a few words.

Gen. Charles P. Stone commanded what he called a corps of observation, on the Maryland side of the Potomac River. His pickets extended from the mouth of the Monocacy, on the north, to meet with those of Banks' division on the south. Stone occupied Poolsville as his headquarters. Between the 20th and 22d of October Gen. McCall had advanced from the Army of the Potomac on the right bank of that river as far as Drainsville, his object being to ascertain the number and intentions of the enemy at Leesburg. In co-operating with this movement Gen. Stone sent a large force to Edward's Ferry, and increased the command at Harrison's Island. At Edward's Ferry, three miles from Poolsville, Gen. Stone made a feint of crossing the river, on the 20th, at one o'clock, P. M. Several boat-loads of troops crossed and recrossed, lines of troops were deployed on the Maryland shore, as if preparatory to embarkation, while batteries opened with shells upon a regiment of the enemy's infantry that appeared from the direction of Leesburg.

Between six and seven P. M. of the same day, Lieut. Church Howe, Quartermaster of the Fifteenth Massachusetts Regiment, commanded by Col. Charles Devens, was seen crossing the river from Harrison's Island to the Maryland shore, where, mounting his horse, he galloped rapidly away in the direction of Edward's Ferry. At this time the Island was occupied by one company of Col. Devens's regiment, commanded by Capt. Philbrick. From Poolsville to the Potomac opposite Harrison's Island is about five miles. From the Maryland to the Virginia shore at this point is 4,290 feet, or a little over three fourths of a mile. In the middle of the river is Harrison's Island; where the troops crossed it, it is about 1,650 feet in width, and this leaves for the river itself, between the Maryland shore and the Island, a width of 1,320 feet: to the Virginia shore from the Island the width is about the same.

Earlier in the day, at about two P. M., Col. Lee, commanding the Twentieth Massachusetts Regiment, in camp near Poolsville, received orders from Gen. Stone to proceed with all his command, save a camp-guard, to the tow-path of the canal opposite Harrison's Island, where he would receive further orders. At six P. M., Col. Lee, with 318 men, arrived at the place designated. About one hour (to wit, at seven P. M.) after Lee's arrival, Col. Devens, with four companies of his regiment, arrived at the same point, and immediately began throwing them over to the Island. This was effected by a scow that carried forty men at a trip, and by a yawl that would hold eight or ten men besides the rowers. The scow was hauled across by a line between the Maryland shore and the Island. Up to this time troops had been moved with a general view of co-operation from Harrison's Island; but Gen. Stone, in his official report, does not claim that any plan of action had been determined on, or that it was his intention to cross into Virginia from that Island. It probably was not. It is fair to assume that Quartermaster Church Howe initiated the movement. At ten o'clock at night this officer reappeared at the tow-path opposite Harrison's Island, bearing dispatches from Gen. Stone to Col. Devens. These dispatches were unsealed, and as they came first by Col. Lee, that officer read them by the light of a pine torch. Col. Devens was ordered to cross from Harrison's Island into Virginia in the course of the night. Why and for what, appears from Gen. Stone's official report, in which he says, "At ten P. M. (it was probably a little earlier), Lieut. Howe, Quartermaster of the Fifteenth Massachusetts, reported that scouts under Capt. Philbrick had returned to the Island, having been within one mile of Leesburg, and there discovered on the edge of the woods an encampment of thirty tents; that there were no pickets out; and that he (Capt. Philbrick) approached to within twenty-five rods without being even challenged."

It is not known by whose orders this movement was made by Capt. Philbrick. Gen. Stone does not report that it was made by his orders. Was it through Church Howe's zeal? So far as it appears, so important a movement, one that involved such serious consequences, is without a responsible father.

The order then continued: Col. Devens would march silently under cover of night to the position of the camp referred to, attack and destroy it at daybreak, pursue the enemy lodged there as far as would be prudent, and return immediately to the Island. Col. Devens was further ordered to make close observation of the position, strength, and movements of the enemy; but in the event of there being no enemy there visible, to hold on in a secure position until he could be strengthened sufficiently to make a valuable reconnoissance. To replace the troops on Harrison's Island, thus to be used by Col. Devens, Col. Lee was ordered to cross his command over to the Island, and further received orders to send one hundred men to the Virginia side of the river, where he was to occupy the bluffs on its immediate shore, and cover the retreat of Col. Devens, should he be obliged to fall back. Col. Lee's whole command was three hundred and eighteen men. At the same time, apparently in contemplation of turning Devens's movement into a reconnoissance, orders were sent to Col. Baker, commanding a regiment called the First California, to send that regiment to Conrad's Ferry, to arrive there at sunrise of the 21st, and have the remainder of his brigade ready to move early. The remainder of the Fifteenth Regiment, under command of Lieut.-Col. Wood, was also ordered to be on the tow-path of the canal opposite Harrison's Island at daybreak. Two mountain howitzers, in charge of Lieut. French, of Ripley's Battery, were also ordered to be at the same place at the same time. Towards morning of the 21st, Col. Devens began the crossing of his five companies. All told, his force numbered three hundred and fifty men. The means available for crossing were two boats, one a metallic life-boat, capable of carrying ten or twelve men at a time, the other a common flat-bottomed boat, used for ducking purposes, and capable of carrying from six to eight men if closely stowed. In two or three hours, Col. Devens with his command had been transferred to the Virginia shore. Then Col. Lee, with two companies, numbering one hundred and one men, crossed for the duty designated in the order. It was about five o'clock in the morning of the 21st of October, not yet daylight. From the water's edge the bluff rose at an angle of 30° for one hundred feet before reaching the plateau above. Climbing the zizzag foot-path, Col. Lee reported to Col. Devens that his command was in position. Directly in their front, and less than two miles and a half away, was Leesburg. An indistinct cart-path, some ten or twelve feet in width, led towards it.

Along this path, through the woods, Col. Devens started at once to execute his orders. Col. Lee then covered his own front and flanks with small scouting parties, composed of a non-commissioned officer and two men to each. It was half-past seven A. M. when firing was heard on Col. Lee's right rear, — a half-dozen discharges, — and the sergeant of the party came in wounded. A half an hour later a regular volley was heard in front, succeeded by an irregular fire, the whole over in a few minutes, after which wounded men from Col. Devens's command made their appearance on the cart-path, emerging from the woods in front. The attack upon Col. Lee's scouting party and upon Col. Devens's battalion was by a single company of the Seventeenth Regiment Mississippi Infantry, commanded by a Capt. Duff. On the Saturday previous, this company, which had been on picket duty on the Virginia shore, had been sent to Harper's Ferry, and now, returning to resume its duty and reinstate the pickets, stumbled first upon the unexpected scouts of Lee, whom, carefully reconnoitering, they plumped squarely upon Devens with his command in line, and fired, receiving the return volley described.

Nothing more happened until about nine o'clock, when Col. Devens's battalion appeared, marching by a flank. The command halted in the open space occupied by Col. Lee, and there they remained about twenty minutes, when Col. Devens said to Col. Lee that he intended to return again to the front for the purpose of recovering his dead; saying which, he again at once disappeared, removing to his former position, which was between a half mile and a mile from the bluff. Very early in the morning, before any firing had taken place, Col. Devens had found that the scouts had been deceived as to an enemy's camp; in the uncertain light they had mistaken openings between trees for tents. Inasmuch, then, as Col. Devens had not found the enemy he expected, he seems to have remained where he was, in pursuance of the final part of Gen. Stone's order, "to hold on in a secure position until he could be strengthened sufficiently to make a valuable reconnoissance." Soon after the return of Col. Devens, Quartermaster Church Howe again appeared upon the scene. Crossing from Harrison's Island and climbing the bluff, and saying that he came as one of Gen. Stone's staff officers, he inquired of Col. Lee about the position. Col. Lee told him to report to Gen. Stone, that the troops ordered by him into Virginia had occupied the river shore; that they numbered about four hundred men; that Col. Devens had about thirty rounds of ammunition for each man, and that Col. Lee had forty rounds; that the troops were without subsistence; and that if the Government designed to fight a battle and occupy the Virginia shore permanently, reinforcements, with commissary and subsistence stores, were necessary. Lieut. Church Howe desired Col. Lee to go with him to see Col. Devens, but that officer replied that his orders required him to hold the bluff to cover the retreat of Col. Devens, and that he could not leave; upon which Quartermaster Howe went to the front alone: soon reappearing with an escort, he recrossed the river. Howe reported to Stone, as soon as he could reach him, that Col. Devens had found no enemy — meaning, probably, no tents — as reported, but that he had concealed his force in a piece of woods, and was examining the space between that and Leesburg. Stone at once ordered a non-commissioned officer with ten cavalrymen to report to Devens, "to scour the country." At the same time he ordered Lieut.-Col. Ward to cross into Virginia with the remaining companies of the Fifteenth Regiment, "move to the right, on to Smart's mills, to protect Devens's flank," when he should return; and "secure a crossing more favorable than the first, and connected by a good road with Leesburg." As ordered, the cavalry, — numbering, however, only six men, — with Capt. Candy, Assistant Adjutant-General on Gen. Lander's staff, in command, came across the river and joined Col. Lee on the bluff. At this time there had been no change in affairs. The cavalry, without performing its designated duty, having proceeded no further than the bluff, went back again to the Maryland side. By eight o'clock in the morning of the 21st, Major Revere, of the Twentieth Massachusetts Regiment, had succeeded in getting the scow that Col. Devens had used as a transport from the Maryland shore to Harrison's Island around the north part of the Island, for use in transporting troops to the Virginia shore. This was of material aid in crossing the additional troops. It was now between half-past eleven and twelve A. M. Some rations of hard bread and pork and fifty empty boxes had been sent to Col. Lee. The officer who brought the latter told the Colonel they were to be filled with earth and laid up to form an entrenched position. Col. Lee ordered the two mountain howitzers, under command of Lieut. French, of Co. I, First United States Artillery, to be sent over; and as they had been ordered to report to him on the 20th, and were then on Harrison's Island, they came immediately. Between half-past twelve and one o'clock, Lieut.-Col. Ward, with the remainder of the Fifteenth Massachusetts Regiment, appeared on the Virginia bluff, and immediately proceeded to the front to join Col. Devens, instead of executing the orders of Gen. Stone.

We now return to Col. Baker, who, having accompanied the California Regiment to the tow-path off Harrison's Island, proceeded in person to Edward's Ferry, and reported to Gen. Stone that the remainder of his brigade was ready to march. He was ordered to Harrison's Island to assume command. Gen. Stone says in his report that he was "anxious to ascertain the exact position and force of the enemy in our front, and to explore as far as it was safe on the right towards Leesburg, and on the left towards Leesburg and the gum-spring road." Col. Baker was to judge, so Stone says, of the sufficiency of the mode of crossing the river into Virginia with his command, which might consist, if he desired to use them, of all the troops under Cols. Devens and Lee, and in addition the guns of a section each of Vaughn's and Bunting's Batteries, and all the troops of his own brigade; and Gen. Stone continues, "I left it to his discretion, after viewing the ground, to retire from the Virginia shore under cover of his guns and the fire of the large infantry force, or to pass over reinforcements in case he found it practicable and the position on the other side favorable. If he passed artillery across the river, he was to see it supported by good infantry; and I pointed out to him the position of bluffs on this side the river from which artillery could act with effect on the other; and leaving the matter of crossing more troops or retiring what were already over to his discretion, I gave him entire control of operations on the right. This gallant and energetic officer left me about nine A. M., or half-past nine, and galloped off quickly to his command." And again says Stone: "Messengers from Harrison's Island informed me, soon after the arrival of Col. Baker, that he was crossing his whole force as rapidly as possible, and that he had caused an additional flat-boat to be rafted from the canal, into the river."*

About one o'clock, P. M., Col. Baker, making his appearance on the bluff, inquired for Col. Lee, to whom, as he was pointed out, he introduced himself as "Col. Baker." "Have you reported to take command?" inquired Col. Lee. "I have," Col. Baker replied, and then added, "And I congratulate you, sir, upon a battle upon the soil of Virginia." Col. Baker then asked as to the whereabouts of Col. Devens, and was told that he was half a mile or more in front of that position. Asking for a volunteer to communicate with him, a sergeant stepped out, and was sent off with a message directing Col. Devens to fall back to the bluff. About this time one field-piece drawn by six horses, a piece of a R. I. Battery, in charge of Lieut. Branhall, of the Ninth N. Y. Battery, came upon the field. The gun was unlimbered, horses and limber passed to the rear, to the edge of the bluff, a distance of forty or fifty feet. Between twelve and one o'clock the enemy had appeared in some force in front of Devens, and a sharp skirmish had ensued. Being unsupported, the Colonel had fallen back to a piece of woods about half a mile in front of Lee's position on the bluff, and here he remained unmolested until he fell back, as ordered.

---

* To take the place of the one removed by Major Revere to the west side of the Island during the night.

Col. Baker, dismounting from his horse and hanging his cape cloak upon a tree, now proceeded to form his line of battle. As the Fifteenth came in, moving by companies, he formed his right centre on the north of the cart-path, and parallel to it. It consisted of the Fifteenth Massachusetts Regiment and one company of the Twentieth Massachusetts. A portion of this line, thrown back on its right at a right angle to the main body, consisting of three companies of the Fifteenth Massachusetts and the company of the Twentieth Massachusetts, was under the command of Major Kimball, of the Fifteenth. The six-pounder gun, with a portion of the Twentieth Massachusetts Regiment and two companies of the California Regiment, constituted the centre; while a little in advance and perpendicular to the cart-path on its southerly side, two other companies of the California Regiment, two of the Forty-Second New York, and one of the Twentieth Massachusetts, under command of Lieut.-Col. Wistar, of the Californians, made the left wing in the line of battle. Three companies of the Twentieth Massachusetts Regiment constituted the reserve; they were opposite the centre and close to the edge of the bluff. Seven companies of Col. Lee's regiment were in the fight. The mountain howitzers were placed on the right of the main body of the Fifteenth Massachusetts, under Col. Devens. These dispositions made, Col. Baker, turning to Col. Lee, asked, "How do you like my line of battle?" — "I think it should be made upon our left on the brink of that ravine," replied Col. Lee. To this suggestion Baker made no reply. A narrow and deep ravine, running diagonally from the direction of the cart-path towards the river, seemed not only to offer an impassable obstacle to the enemy, but somewhat served as a cover in case it became necessary to retire upon Edward's Ferry, where Stone was then operating. As Baker formed his line of battle, the enemy could have come in between the brink of the ravine and our left wing. Since morning the enemy had been drawing nearer and nearer, feeling Baker's position and ascertaining his numbers. The skirmish with Devens, and a few shells fired from the Heights on the Maryland shore which reached their columns, did not retard his advance. It was now between half-past one and two P. M. This was the hour when the enemy came in on the front and right,— the Eighth Virginia Regiment immediately in the front, a battalion of the Thirteenth Mississippi, and Cudworth's Cavalry dismounted on the right. The cavalry numbered about three hundred. The Eighth Virginia came to the edge of the woods bordering the open space within which was formed the centre of Baker's line of battle, and halting, formed in line, about two hundred and fifty feet from the line. The Virginians certainly, as well as the men of the Fifteenth Massachusetts Regiment, and perhaps others, were armed with smooth-bore muskets.

And so the battle commenced. It will be perceived that our line was in the form of a curtain, running towards the ravine, but not reaching it on the left, and terminating on the right in an angle, the face of which was formed by the Fifteenth Massachusetts, under command of Devens and Kimball. The six-pounder gun opened fire at once upon the Eighth Virginia, so did the supporting force of infantry; while at the same time Major Kimball opened fire on the Mississippians and the dismounted cavalry. The gun in the centre was loaded and fired with energy, but being provided with neither grape nor canister it was almost useless. At an expenditure of moments most precious, boats had been used to bring to the field a field-piece and six horses, with a limber filled with James' percussion shells. Not an ounce of grape could be found, though Col. Lee searched for it, as he was with his own hands conveying these shells to the gun. It was not fifteen minutes from the time the enemy made their appearance before every man at the field-piece, save one sergeant, was shot down. So withering was the fire that the two companies of Californians supporting the right of the centre laid down flat upon the ground. Entreaties, violence, and sword-cuts by Col. Baker and his officers could not prevail upon them; and so early in the action they went to the rear without participating in the fight. When they retreated, two companies of the reserve were ordered up to take their places and support the gun. They came, and in a few moments officers and men were nearly destroyed; they were of the Twentieth Massachusetts. While this contest was going on in the centre, Major Kimball, on the right, had been obliged to fall back. On the left, Lt.-Col. Wistar had been wounded, and the fight was progressing languidly on our side, being continued by detached companies. Our ammunition was giving out; some men of the Twentieth were supplying themselves from the cartridge-boxes of the slain. The enemy now showed himself in strong numbers on our left. The Seventeenth and Eighteenth Mississippi and a battalion of the Thirteenth Mississippi came into line of battle parallel to the south brink of the ravine and near its edge; and here they opened a destructive fire on our left. At the same time the Eighth Virginia advanced out of the wood, in line of battle, upon Baker's centre, and the Mississippians and Cudworth's dismounted cavalry were pressing up on his right. The Union troops were in a square, the front, right and left sides of which were held by the enemy, while directly in their rear was the steep bluff, falling to a swollen and unfordable river. It was now that Col. Lee said to Col. Baker, "Sir, the day is going hard with us," to which Col. Baker replied, "The battle is lost, sir." Then, as if unwilling to survive it, this brave man moved forward to the front, down the cart-path, or nearly on its line, and there, in the front of the left of his line, he fell riddled with bullets. So near was he to the Eighth Virginia Regiment that Col. Lee saw a tall officer step out to within ten paces and deliver with his pistol his fire at Col. Baker's head; at the same time, from a squad, a volley of musketry was fired at him, when he fell to rise no more. As some of the Californians carried his body to the rear, Col. Lee saw on the side of his head where the pistol-shot of the officer had taken effect. He was carried across the river into Maryland, as narrated, and we had passed the house which held his dead body. After the death of Col. Baker, Col. Lee conferred with Col. Devens and Major Revere and one or two other officers. What was to be done? There seemed to be no answer; so Col. Lee, as commanding officer, took upon himself the responsibility, and gave orders to fall back upon the river shore, under the bluff. But at this moment Capt. Hardy, the Assistant Adjutant-General of Col. Baker, appeared with Col. Cogswell. Col. Cogswell, commanding a Tammany regiment of Baker's Brigade, had managed to cross during the fight, and now, claiming to be the ranking officer among the survivors, directed an attempt to be made to open communication with Edward's Ferry. Col. Lee instantly acceded, saying it was no time to discuss rank, that he would obey Col. Cogswell's orders; and orders were then given to move by the left flank. About two hundred men, being portions of the Fifteenth and Twentieth Massachusetts regiments and of the Forty-Second New York, obeyed the order; but when they arrived at the brink of the ravine they received a volley at short range from one of the Mississippi regiments in line on the opposite brink, and they fell back to the place from whence they started. And now the Eighth Virginia Regiment slowly advanced. The few Union troops that had preserved their formation were formed in line of battle to oppose them. Col. Lee, with ten or twelve officers and between twenty and thirty men, fell back to the river-side, down the bluff. The enemy instantly rushed forward to the edge of the bluff, where, without any obstacle, their fire commanded the passage of the river. The bank was lined with the dead and wounded. Boats filled with wounded were still passing from the Virginia shore to Harrison's Island; and these boats were a scow, the life-boat, and the little ducking boat. The whole of these boats were capable of carrying at one time from forty-six to fifty men.

Hardly had this scene of horrors opened to the enemy when, with yells of exultation, they piled horror on horror. They fired volley upon volley into the struggling wretches who had leaped into the chilling waters of the Potomac; they riddled the scow, filled as she was with dead and dying, — they riddled it with bullets, and it sank with its dying and its dead, sank in the middle of the stream. Crossing the river from the Island, empty and sculled by a single oarsman, the metallic life-boat met their gaze; the oarsman was instantly shot, and the boat drifted idly down the stream; there was nothing left but the little ducking boat, and that was now useless. There was nothing left but to swim, surrender, or die. "With a devotion worthy the cause they were serving," says Gen. Stone in his official report, "officers and men, while quarter was being offered to such as would lay down their arms, stripped themselves of their swords and muskets, and hurled them out into the river to prevent their falling into the hands of the foe, and saved themselves as they could by swimming, floating on logs, and concealing themselves in the bushes of the forest, to make their way up and down the river bank to a place of crossing." Col. Devens escaped by swimming. Col. Lee, in attempting to make his way up the river, was, with Major Revere and some of his other officers, captured in the woods in the middle of the night by the enemy's cavalry; taken to Leesburg, he there found himself in the presence of the rebel commander who had whipped him, — a Gen. N. G. Evans, of South Carolina, a graduate of West Point, familiarly known as Shanks Evans from the peculiar formation of his legs, which were very knock-kneed. Col. Lee says it was hard to tell which of the two, Cogswell or Evans, both having been old friends in the old army, was the more overcome at the meeting. Evans had invited his unwilling guest to join him in a convivial draught of peach brandy, and Cogswell was saying to his conqueror, "I tell ye, Shanks, shan't take my parole on any such terms; I'll see you d—d first, Shanks." Gen. Evans had offered to release Col. Cogswell if he would sign a parole not to fight again during the war, and this the Colonel was refusing to do. Owing to the peach brandy, the refusal was given in strong terms. Col. Lee also, but more politely, rejected Gen. Evans's proffer. So our prisoners went to Richmond, to be afterwards exchanged. If Col. Lee could have found anything to float on, or if the raft which he and his officers tried to buckle together with their belts would have floated, they might have crossed without trouble. The loss in killed in this fight has never been accurately ascertained; a large number were shot in the river while trying to swim. The report of the rebel commander gives as their number engaged 3,500 men, being four regiments of infantry and a battalion of cavalry. Col. Lee's memorandum of the forces engaged on our side, taken as they came up and reported on the bluff for duty, was 1,603 men. Five hundred and twenty, including the wounded, were captured. The battle lasted from two P. M. until ten minutes before six, at which time Col. Lee ordered his command to retire down the bank.

It does not seem necessary to spend much time in conclusions. The means of transportation from the Maryland shore to the Island, and from thence to the Virginia shore, I have given. With such means not over three hundred an hour could have been added to our force under the most favorable circumstances: how much less with the returning wounded and the depression of probable defeat! Gen. Stone says in his comments, "The forwarding of artillery before its supporting force of infantry also impeded the rapid assembling of an imposing force on the Virginia shore. If the infantry forces had first crossed, a difference of one thousand men would have been made in the infantry line at the time of attack, probably enough to have given us the victory. If any officers or men were charged with the duty of ensuring the regular passage of troops, it was not performed ; for the reinforcements, as they arrived, found no one in command of the boats, and great delays were occasioned."

Col. Baker expiated his fault with his life. He was a brave and energetic man. As a Senator in the United States Senate from Oregon, he had deemed it necessary to make public speeches upon the conduct of the war ; from the Pacific to the Atlantic he had condemned the slowness of McClellan's movements, and criticised what he interpreted to be his disinclination to fight. Full of courage and of vanity, he lost sight of the elements which make success possible in such undertakings as he lent himself to achieve. But just from a confidential interview with President Lincoln, where he had expressed himself as in entire sympathy with the President's feelings at the manner in which McClellan was delaying, and held out hopes that should an opportunity offer he would startle the country with what a fighting commander could accomplish, he saw opening before him his opportunity. The large powers intrusted to him by Gen. Stone, he never thought of using other than for a fight, and when, too late, he saw his error, he expiated it with his life. Would that some others had done likewise, and that the enemy had captured their commissions as major-general as the enemy captured Baker's, when they found his cape overcoat hanging on a tree, at the time his body was lying stark and stiff in Maryland.

The demonstration from Edward's Ferry by Gen. Stone was not so serious as to call for the use of much, if any, of Gen. Evans's force to observe it. Gen. Stone could not aid Col. Baker, so he says, by marching along the Virginia shore, because " there was a rebel battery in the woods between the two ferries, which had prevented a reconnoissance in that direction."

At four P. M. a telegram from Gen. Stone to Gen. Banks, for a brigade to occupy the Maryland shore opposite Harrison's Island, had caused our movement, as I have narrated. Our brigade was to replace those troops at Conrad's Ferry which Gen. Stone then supposed to be pressing on victorious after the flying rebels. Hence the letter to me that Gen. Stone was in Leesburg, with very little fighting. At five o'clock, P. M., news of Col. Baker's death was conveyed to Gen. Stone; the news of the disaster soon followed. Instructions delivered on the road from Gen. Stone met Gen. Hamilton: these were, to repair to Conrad's Ferry, and there dispose of his force so as to protect Harrison's Island.

The rain poured piteously upon us all day of the 22d, as all day fugitives and wounded came into our lines. Parts of three regiments were utterly demoralized and routed, and yet there was a plucky feeling among some. A bright youth of the Fifteenth Massachusetts Regiment, from Worcester, looked longingly at a miserable fire, trying to burn in my favor despite the rain; a soldier's overcoat covered him, — his remaining garments were in Virginia.

"Where did you come from, my man?" I asked.

"Virginny," he replied.

Somehow or other he took a long pull at my whiskey flask. How his eyes twinkled as he returned it with thanks!

Yes, he did have a hard time. Col. Devens told him to take care of himself; he (the colonel) was going to swim.

"When are you ready to go back again?"

"Just as soon as I can get another suit of clothes," he said, with unmistakable emotion.

The movement was over. For two or three days we extended our guards along the Potomac, and once we marched to Edward's Ferry and crossed the river into Virginia, only to turn round, recross, and march back again. We suffered now from over caution, — a penalty for the want of it.

Our troops were again all on the Maryland side of the Potomac. Gen. McClellan had visited us and departed.

On the 26th of October, at nine o'clock, A. M., our regiment turned its face again towards Darnstown, and on the 27th, after two days of marching, away back in some Maryland farmer's field, skirted by wood on the north and east, out of sight of the highway and in sight of the Potomac, we made our encampment; we were about four miles from our old camp. Here the days were a constant repetition of drum-beat and drill, orders from headquarters, picket duty, cold weather, rain, hurricane, smoky tents, old newspapers, military tribulations, vague hopes, and more vague instruction by a topographical engineer officer, on Gen. Banks' staff, in some details of field engineering. Here the Sibley tents proved themselves worthy of their reputation; for they held in warmth and in comfort some sixteen or seventeen soldiers in each, around a fire beneath the iron tripod that supported the single pole, while the smoke curled out of a hole at the top. Here, too, we received two thousand pairs of stockings from Mrs. Harrison Gray Otis, one thousand pairs collected in ten days, votive offerings for our regiment. Some of them were from the young ladies at Prof. Agassiz's school, at Cambridge, and these were like the world when it was without form and void; some were from Campton Village, in New Hampshire, with names of knitters stitched on them, and they were of colors red, white, and blue, and there were prizes in them, — pin-cushions, needle-cases, Life of Havelock, the *real* Christian soldier, moral tracts, and much that tended to make the knapsack heavier on many a weary march. Poor fellows! how many were to struggle onward under that weary load, but at last to expose to some stranger's eye the little Bible or the dear letter or the loving token from a home the soldier never more shall gaze upon. Friend or foe, whoever he may be, the heart will ache for such in sympathy. Said an Indiana colonel to me at this camp, "Some of my boys shot some of the enemy's pickets; they got their knapsacks, and found them filled with letters from home and nice things beautifully made by the Southern women."

Hardly had we arrived at this camp when Capt. Cary made application to me for permission to cross the river and get reliable intelligence of the missing in the recent massacre at Ball's Bluff. I gave my assent, moved by the feeling that it might bring relief to fathers and mothers, to wives and children, to know that some of the absent of the fight were held as prisoners, and not dead beneath the waters of the Potomac. In addition to my assent, I wrote a letter to Gen N. G. Evans, the rebel commander. It was well known at the time that Capt. Cary's effort terminated without result. The captain crossed, but found no one within two miles of the river on the Virginia side. With a white handkerchief on the end of a stick, in token of his peaceful designs, Capt. Cary at last encountered a non-belligerent Irishman, who informed him that if he should come across any of the enemy's guerillas, that white rag would n't do him any good. "And that," said the captain, when he reported to me, "was about the conclusion I had come to; so I concluded to return."

Every day now made it more and more apparent that winter was upon us. Huge fires of logs in front of our tents ceased to convey any warmth inside; we had no stoves; holes a foot deep and three feet long, with a flat stone on top, served as fire-places; the wood entered at one end, the smoke escaped by the aid of three flour-barrels as a chimney outside the tent at the other. But what were tents in such days and nights of rain and wind on that Muddy Branch? Our tents were often prostrated, our encampment a mass of shapeless canvas. On the 2d of November we were treated to a hurricane, with rain. A huge oak branch, torn off by the storm, fell athwart my tent, snapping the ridge-pole like a pipe-stem; luckily, I had just stepped out to attend reveille. More than one half of the officers' tents were down; the parade-ground became a miniature ocean; the rain pelted the canvas; the tent-cords strained and tugged at their fastenings; while, like discharges of small arms, the canvas cracked, and the wind roared in volleys through the tree-tops. The sentinels crouched under the storm, with their rifles under their arms, and their shoulders covered with overcoats and india-rubber blankets. It was a hard time for the healthy ; it was a sorry encampment for the sick. Lieut.-Col. Andrews prostrated with typhoid fever in an adjoining house, and our hospital tents filled with men suffering from the measles, now an epidemic, contributed to the dismal miseries of Muddy Branch. It was about this time, too, that the fleet sailed for South Carolina, to make a first attempt at landing. Every blast of the tempest threatened its destruction.

On the 8th of November, during a brief absence of fifteen days, the command of our regiment devolved upon Wilder Dwight. In characteristic letters he informed me of the condition of the regiment, and that he had moved it to higher ground, near Seneca Creek. But the weather would not change with the encampment. " It is a raw and gusty night," he writes ; "the troubled Potomac is undoubtedly chafing with his shores, and although this first taste of winter agrees with our men, it is not favorable to admirable precision in drill ; " news of the fleet landing at Beaufort, S. C., "makes him jolly ; " Gen. Banks tells him that he " feels the whole division will be moved soon," and Copeland has returned from Washington with gossip "that we are to form part of an expedition." " Can't you get us ordered South ? " he then asks. " Wish you could see McClellan, and get us out of this latitude and atmosphere into one of warmer activity ; it is cold up here," he adds. Then he speaks of Thanksgiving, — " Gov. Andrew would like to have it observed, and he has sent on his proclamation, psalms and all." Then there are other items. " Col. Andrews is still sick ; his wife came on Sunday ; the measles are diminishing ; " he has a " comfortable shelter for my horse ; gets on with drills respectably, though he can understand an occasional gentle hint to ——. Col. Webster commands the brigade ; the new officers have not come," and he is preparing to "celebrate Thanksgiving"; also, that "Lieut. J. M. Ellis has resigned, having received an appointment as captain in the commissary department of the volunteer service."

On the 28th of November I returned again to camp, bringing with me as visitors from Boston Messrs. Thomas Motley, W. R. Robeson, and E. F. Bowditch. Our camp, though higher and dryer, was a cheerless spot. Though there were only ten or a dozen cases of measles in the hospital, two or three new ones presented themselves every day, while by day or night sounds of distressing colds and coughs were audible. No watchfulness could ward off sickness, or remove that condition which offered such temptations to disease when the right kind presented itself. My hospital tents were crowded, and thirty men sick in their tents. The commissioned officers did not escape, — Capts. Savage and Mudge, and Lieut. Wheaton were seriously ill in houses. We had fires in tents, in stoves received about the first of December. I did all I could to make the men comfortable. It was the 13th day of December before we received information that this wretched spot was to know us no more, that we were going to remove to the much healthier locality of Frederick. So our sick were sent to Washington by the canal.

How over one hundred and fifty or two hundred poor fellows, typhoid and bilious fever patients, and patients with fractures and ills grievous to be borne, after waiting from 9 A. M. till 4 P. M., were huddled into the damp hold of a common canal boat, for the hospitals at Washington, — a hold in which there was not as much provision as the most indifferent teamster provides for his horse, even straw to lie down upon, until I ordered some to be procured; and how all the unfortunates could not be taken at that single trip, but were hauled home to be hauled back again next day, save some too sick who were transferred to an adjoining store, where at night one man died; how when these poor men reached Washington they laid two days in the boat before being removed to the hospital, and during this time had only water crackers to eat ; and how the whole story was told in the "Boston Post," *to persuade others to enlist*, is a part of our history I do not like to recall. And as well for this, among many other reasons, because it brings before me again that poor boy Kittredge, of Lowell, a recruit, and therefore a fit subject for that scourge among new soldiers, typhoid fever, with which I found him greatly emaciated in our canvas hospital. Too sick to move with the others, I ordered our surgeon to remove him to Darnstown and place him in the church, used as a hospital. After we left, by an order, this poor boy was removed five or six miles to the canal, thence by boat to Point of Rocks, thence by rail to Frederick, where he arrived to die, soon after his arrival. It is said his feet were frozen upon the passage.

On Tuesday morning, the 3d day of December, we turned our backs willingly upon the dismal camp at Seneca Creek and Muddy Branch, and making that day seventeen and one half miles, encamped at night at the small town of Barnsville, *en route* to Frederick.

A patch of woods in the outskirts of Barnsville was our halting place for the night. When the men were comfortable before their huge fires, and tents and camp-kettles ; when the horses were fed and sheltered as well as I could contrive, then with the chaplain, major, and quartermaster I started for the aristocratic town of Barnsville ; for there was a supper awaiting us, ordered by my cook in anticipation of our arrival; a nice supper he said it was. We were positively saturated with hunger. Conceive then of our feelings on finding soldiers filling the house and our supper filling the soldiers. You may rest assured there were no men of the Second among them ; they were all from other regiments of the brigade. Headquarters of the Second took possession of a bedroom, ordered a second supper, which never appeared. With fifty or more famished officers at the headquarters of the brigade, late at night, hunger was satisfied with twenty-five cents' worth of food ; it was all the lady of the mansion would accept, and all she ought to demand. It was fifteen minutes after four in the morning when reveille sounded. It was dark ; the campfires roared among the trees, and the stars twinkled in the sky, as the soldiers, hurrying to and fro in the ruddy glare, prepared their breakfasts. At five o'clock the drum sounded, "Strike your tents!" and tents fell simultaneously. Wagons packed, horses hitched up, the first streak of dawn saw our regiment moving out of the wood, along the road to Frederick. The thermometer was far below the freezing point, but the roads were in good order, the men inspirited. We were to lead the brigade, provided no other regiment caught us ; therefore I ordered the regiment to do its best. We made sixteen miles in four and one half hours, nine of them without a halt. I know how much this march tired a foot man, for I walked the whole of it. My orderly led my horse. We did lead the brigade to Frederick, and there, in its outskirts, we passed the night ; and next day, the 5th of December, notwithstanding the assurances of Gen. Banks to me that it was not the intention to put our army into winter quarters, only to place them where they could be moved easily by rail, we went into winter quarters, and remained until the 27th day of February, in the year 1862.

On the turnpike, towards Baltimore, about three miles from Frederick City, in Maryland, turn to the left and follow for a few rods a small stream, and it will lead to a fine growth of timber, which, gently falling away towards the south, opens upon a grassy field. In these woods and upon this slope was located the camp of our regiment. The underbrush was cleared away, and trees that interfered with the regularity of our camp cut down. The wood became a delightful grove, where the sun shone all day, to the great improvement of health.

Frederick City, with its nine thousand inhabitants sheltered in real houses, with its civilizing influences, the result of some centuries of experience, found itself surrounded by some seventeen thousand men cradled elsewhere, — men getting along with nature in the rough, canvas for houses, straw and a blanket for a bed, the grove for a church and the drum for church-bells: with these and a few other artificial appliances, we invited the citizens of Frederick to see how comfortable we could become when we fell back upon first principles. But we were not going into winter quarters, we were told; this was to deceive those who, shouting onward! remained behind; therefore we went into winter quarters by jerks. Boards for tent floors came first; then we ventured on sides, built up about three feet high, in which there was a slide door; upper sides and roofs of canvas, that is, we pitched our tents on top. At length, it was on the 17th of December, an order came to estimate for lumber for huts: we were to remain till spring. Cantonment Hicks, as Gen. Abercrombie baptized the encampment of his brigade, in honor of Governor Hicks of Maryland, became our winter quarters.

By the last of December it became apparent that we were in winter quarters in truth. Sometimes the grounds were white with snow, and the parade ground obliterated; then the sentinels ploughed along in their endless tramp; then the trees stretched their long branches weirdly against a leaden sky, while the men flitted idly from tent to tent, enjoying the cheer and the release from drill. That was a camp of comfort: perhaps there never was another like it; the smoke curled out of the top of a hundred Sibley tents, indicating the genial fire within, and furnishing food for reflection in following winters, when four pieces of thin cotton, each about the dimensions of a good-sized pocket-handkerchief, furnished shelter for four men. And there was the goodly cottage in which dwelt the colonel of the regiment. Verily, the men builded better than I intended. The huge chestnut logs that formed the walls were each drawn from the forest by four horses; from these walls sprung oaken rafters, upon which was thrown a covering of tarred paper, battened down, for a roof; and then the fire-place within, — a huge opening of brick, where great logs of dry oak crackled, and the flames leaped with laughter up my wide-mouthed chimney, and the fiery sparks danced along the snowy roof, leaving no footprints of their merry sport.

But we were not altogether idle in that camp at Frederick. As the old year died, and the new moments of the new year were being told off on the dial, the people at home were aroused with astonishment at the latest news, viz. the suspension by the Boston and New York banks of specie payments, while we, utterly regardless of money and its mysteries, were perfecting ourselves in the duties of a soldier. For this there were all sorts of regulations and requirements: it required a mental effort to know how to get out of camp, and where, and when; attempts to enter and supply intoxicating drinks to the troops were guarded against, while for all proper persons restraints were as light as possible. And then there was that daily duty report, recording the attendance of all company officers at the times and places when and where the men were required to do any duty, from a roll-call to a drill, from a company cook's field of operations to the cleanliness of a company street.

The reputation for obedience and discipline which our regiment seemed likely to achieve at Brook Farm, in Massachusetts, was fairly accorded to it in its camp at Frederick. Such results flowed from the recognition of the simple truth that in a soldier's life every hour of the twenty-four has its appropriate duty, and every duty has but one proper mode of performance. To know what that duty was and to see it thoroughly performed was the aim of every commissioned and non-commissioned officer of our regiment, from the colonel down. It was only necessary for the colonel to set the example to observe an enthusiastic and intelligent following. Other regiments of our division, noticing results, attributed them to an unfeeling discipline. The patriarchal relation subsisting between officers and their men in other regiments, in which the colonel was "Old Dad," or "Grandpa," or "Boss," or even "Old Hoss," and the men were "Boys," was unknown to us. Those who recognized the especial *camaraderie* of the volunteers branded us as "Regulars,"—"Gordon's Regulars,"—and this reputation was known throughout the Army of the Potomac. I heard of it in Washington from staff officers of Gen. McClellan; indeed, it was said, as a compliment, we were to be ordered to Washington to guard the city. I trust we were sufficiently thankful for such an escape.

"Is that your colonel?" said a citizen to our chaplain. (I had called at the latter's tent for a moment.)

"It is."

The man looked hard at the chaplain, evidently considering whether a chaplain would romance in that way.

"Certainly it is," repeated the chaplain; adding, "You look incredulous."

"So I am," said the citizen. "I thought Col. Gordon was fifty years old, and as savage as thunder."

Many of you remember the enterprising foreign artist who sold us letter-paper with a pictorial design at the head of each sheet, described underneath as "Camp of the Second Regiment Massachusetts Infantry, at Frederick, Md., Col. George H. Gordon Commanding," in which was represented a sentinel on his post at an *order* arms. There was not a soldier in the brigade that believed that sketch was taken from real life.

I should like to tell of our neighbors, an Indiana regiment of our brigade, who upon an order to march at daylight, afterwards countermanded, yelled vociferously all night and slept all next day; I should like to dwell upon the hospitals, and the drills, and the recitations; but I must not.

There was not much time for play or idleness or disaffection. The men were well fed, thanks to a liberal government; were more than carefully clad, thanks to the Ladies' Association at home; were well sheltered; were well nursed when sick ; were well drilled and disciplined ; were, in short, well cared for when they obeyed, and well punished when they erred ; and so the machine, well regulated, moved under an intelligent will. Notwithstanding the duties of the day, there were times and opportunities for social pleasures at Frederick. That period of intense life found expression in intense feeling, and those people of Frederick who were loyal were so heartily loyal that we never can forget them. The hour of trial for Frederick had not yet come ; but when it did, none of those who invited the Union troops to their houses, who adorned their walls with our regimental flags at their parties, and attended the concerts which our band gave, — none of them ever wavered in their loyalty. God bless Frederick for its true-hearted women! who braved all and suffered all from their devotion to their country.

It was here, at our camp at Frederick, that Gov. Andrew first made known his intention to take the nomination of officers to fill vacancies in our regiment out of my hands. To refer briefly to this matter in giving our history is a necessity : At Maryland Heights, Darnstown, Seneca, and at Frederick, there had been resignations of our officers, — some to enter, with higher rank, the new cavalry regiment forming in Massachusetts, some promoted to staff corps, and some, two or three only, because it was not deemed desirable to retain them. In the record of the Second Massachusetts Infantry Mr. Quint has given the names and rank of those who left us, and the causes which moved them. In filling vacancies in the grade of second lieutenant, it had not occurred to me that the Governor would desire to depart from the plan adopted in the creation of the regiment, — that is, to commission such persons as I might nominate. The appointment, on the 18th of October, of Dr. Leland as surgeon, *vice* Dr. Sargent, resigned through sickness, though without my knowledge or recommendation, inasmuch as it was a medical appointment, I did not consider as laying down a new rule ; nor did the circular letter, dated Nov. 1, 1861, addressed by Gov. Andrew to the colonels of Massachusetts regiments, in which he explained the principles by which he wished to be guided in making appointments to vacancies among the commissioned officers of the Massachusetts volunteer regiments (which duty was imposed upon him by Act of Congress), clearly enunciate a new line of departure. The circular expressed a desire that promotions to fill vacancies should be according to the principle of seniority in rank; while, as for original appointments, it was desired, as a *general rule*, that appointments should be made by "promotions in the regiment in which the vacancy exists." Guided by these rules, the Governor wished colonels of Massachusetts regiments to prepare their recommendations, to be approved by the Commanding General of the brigade, and forwarded to him. I could not conceive these general instructions as departing, in our case, from the original plan, for the reasons given, and therefore looked with apprehension upon being informed by the Governor, on the 13th of December, that he had substituted, for the two young gentlemen whom I had recommended for vacancies among my second lieutenants, two others, then to me unknown. With a certain sense of the fitness of things the War Department had ordered colonels of regiments to test, by military examination, the qualifications of those who were appointed by Governors of States to regiments in the field.

With this power a colonel was master of the situation. In my letter to the Governor, of the 13th of December, I alluded to the actual necessity of commissioning efficient men, insisted that there was no time now to establish a school of instruction, and again presented the names of P. R. Mason and H. B. Scott, to which I added John A. Fox, to fill the vacancy occasioned by the promotion of T. R. Robeson. My gentle hint that those two young gentlemen whom the Governor proposed to send me in the places of my nominees might be severely tested by an examination, brought the reply from the Governor "that he had too much confidence in my honor and integrity to suppose that I would subject officers appointed by him to an examination that I would not subject them to if recommended by myself." In my rejoinder, after reminding the Governor of his promise and action in his original appointments, I claimed that the question of the fitness of any one to receive an appointment in my regiment must ultimately be determined by myself; suggested that possibly a civilian could not judge as well as a soldier of those merits or demerits which make or mar professional fame; doubted much if an experience in the militia would aid discernment; referred to the fact that the War Department had given Mr. Mason a commission since his Excellency's refusal to heed my application for this gentleman; and denied that the opinion of another colonel of a Massachusetts regiment, that Mr. Mason was not qualified to receive a commission in his regiment, should control my wishes to have that gentleman in mine.* I further pointed out to the Governor that he had commissioned citizens whom I had nominated in the places of Captains Curtis, Whitny, and Lieut. Higginson. Astonished therefore at the enunciation of a new policy now, I added, "It is your Excellency's duty to commission officers for my regiment; it is mine to test them. Each act is independent of the will of the other; both may be in harmony." "It is anomalous," I urged, "that the General Government should have placed a commissioning power in the hands of Governors of States, which act begins and ends their responsibility for the appointee, as also the latter's responsibility to them; each meeting but for a moment, part in official relations forever — a new relation subsisting, the responsibilities of which are borne by those who are alone subject to, can receive orders from, and are in every way amenable to another head, that of the War Department. Such have been the wise provisions of law since the organization of this vast army.

---

* This had been urged by the Governor against my nomination of Mr. Mason.

I cannot waive this duty imposed upon me, either as to time or mode of performance."

Then suggesting that there could be but a single motive in the selection of candidates, in either the Governor or myself, and that motive "fitness," I asked his Excellency to submit to me such names as he might desire to appoint in my regiment, and if I was sure they possessed the fitness which "it is made by higher authority than either of us could control my duty to determine," I should certainly not object to his Excellency's appointments. My letter ended as follows : "Allow me to call your Excellency's attention to the fact that there are six vacancies unfilled in my regiment. In some manner they must be filled; their services are indispensable; I am satisfied with the candidates I have proposed. There have been cases in which the United States Government has recognized and paid for the performance of official duty by gentlemen acting as officers without commissions from the Governors of States. This has been done among Pennsylvania Regiments, is being now done in Massachusetts in the organization of a force for operation on the Southern Coast. I trust I shall not be compelled, for the good of the service, to fill my vacancies in a similar manner."

This ended the controversy, and for us most happily. Since leaving Massachusetts there had been eight resignations of officers in our regiment, — resignations, almost without exception, to take a higher rank elsewhere. We had lost Curtis and Higginson and others, as appears in detail in the record of the Second, and we had received as second lieutenants, to fill vacancies, Shelton and Fox and Crowninshield, Oakey and Scott. I repeat, the controversey closed for us most happily; for it gave the regiment, as one of Gov. Andrew's appointees whom I did not nominate, Daniel Oakey; and it gave us, as commissioned officers whom I did nominate, the young gentlemen whose names I have mentioned.

With the commissioning by the Governor of a number of

sergeants whom I recommended for promotion as second lieutenants, the action of the Governor in this matter was entirely acceptable to me so long as I remained Colonel of the Second Massachusetts Regiment; indeed, save that Mr. Stephen M. Weld, of West Roxbury, on the 26th of December, 1861, made application to me, to nominate for a commission in my regiment his son, Stephen M. Weld, Jr., adding that, before applying to the Governor of Massachusetts for a commission, he would like to know that such appointment would be agreeable to me (of which I gave him, by the way, the fullest assurance), this correspondence with the Governor closed the subject. I may mention here that Mr. Weld subsequently concluded to accept an appointment on the staff of Gen. Fitz John Porter.

There was, however, an interference in a new quarter, and formidable in its opposition to discipline: it was a peremptory order from Gen. Banks to release a private soldier of the regiment from confinement in the guard-house at our Frederick camp, and restore him to duty. I think I had a right to assume that one of Gen Banks' old constituents in Massachusetts, a friend, perhaps father, of the soldier in the guard-house, had made a personal appeal for this release, and so it was ordered; but not so obeyed. My remonstrance, in a letter to the Major-General Commanding, sets forth my feelings; policy should not overthrow principle if it could be avoided. Acknowledging the order, I added, under date of Dec. 26, 1861, "The soldier is in my guard-tent, charged with violation of the 46th article of war; no evidence having been submitted to a court-martial, guilt or innocence cannot be affirmed. I have examined the case, and am satisfied that it is proper to submit it to a court. Not intending to violate any lawful order of a commander, and convinced that the enormity of the military offence committed cannot have been fully laid before you, I have ventured to withhold the execution of your order releasing this soldier from confinement until a further communication. I have in my guard-tent, in irons, another soldier of my regiment, charged with sleeping on his post while a sentinel. It is charged that he was found a few paces from his post, asleep and lying down. It is alleged that the private whom you order me to release was found a few paces from his post, asleep and sitting down. Why should one be taken and the other left? Respectfully submitting that I cannot rely upon my sentinels if it happens that a few weeks' or even months' confinement for the commission of this very grave military offence, is followed by a release from arrest and a return to duty, and believing that in this case I have in no manner acted otherwise than is provided in army regulations, and by authority of rules and articles of war, I have the honor respectfully to await further orders in relation to the releasing of this soldier from confinement and restoring him to duty with his company."

I have no record of what became of the subject of this correspondence; but I presume it did no more to mar our amicable relations than it had efficacy in impressing upon Gen. Banks the conviction that he was acting the *rôle* of a General to command, for under date of the 31st of December I find a note from him, addressing me from headquarters, Frederick, Maryland, as "My dear sir," and continuing, "If not any interference with arrangements for your regiment to-morrow, I should esteem it a favor if you would allow your band to visit my headquarters for a couple of hours, say from eleven to one o'clock; for their trouble I will gladly satisfy them.

"Yours very truly,
"N. P. BANKS,
"*M. G. C. Division.*"

On the 16th of February we were anxiously awaiting news from Fort Donaldson. Our line of attack against the Rebellion extended from west to east, almost on a parallel of latitude. Tennessee had been entered; our gunboats had penetrated its rivers even to the northern borders of Alabama; Bowling

Green must be evacuated; Columbus can give no aid to Fort Donaldson, for the latter is invested; Burnside's expedition threatens lines of communication from Manassas. To aid these movements, which have wonderfully raised our spirits, our regiment contributed its quota of fifteen men towards the complement from the Division, — a complement of men to aid in manning the gunboats on Western waters, therefore sailors were wanted. The plan was to gather at Cairo, take Columbus in Tennessee, and then sweep on to New Orleans. To aid in carrying out this magnificent undertaking, Capt. Cary of our regiment was detailed to take the detachment from Banks' Division, and joining a larger command from the Army of the Potomac, proceed with them to Cairo, Ill.

I confess my hopes were somewhat dashed as I read Capt. Cary's first letter from Baltimore, written to me upon his arrival, in which, after writing that he started with sixty-six of the worst men of the Division, nearly all of them drunk, and with no guard but two men, one of whom he begged of the Provost Marshal, he found himself on the way to Baltimore with sixty men of Stone's Division as bad as his own, in charge of Lieut. Raguet, of Gen. Gorman's staff. Having arrived too late to join the main body, which had started, the captain was obliged to put his men in a room, leaving his two reliable men with revolvers at the door of entrance; but alas! upon his return in the morning Capt. Cary found that thirty of his veterans had escaped through a rear door which they had broken open. Obliged to go on with what he had left, he had employed all the police force of Baltimore looking after the absentees. The captain closes with the following mournful revelation: "A policeman told me he had seen hard parties, but this was the worst he ever saw. And this from a Baltimore policeman! You can judge," adds the captain, and continues, "I have tried knocking down, cajoling, wheedling, everything; but they are a set of the most unmitigated d—d scoundrels I ever met. But I can say, when they all get off it will be well for the Division."

Sharp on Capt. Cary's letter came the soul-stirring news that we had captured Fort Donaldson, with more than 15,000 prisoners; that a rebel Gen. Price, with his whole army, had been captured in Arkansas. I was so excited that I ordered the regiment to cheer, the band to play, and I released the officers from recitation for the day. At this time came the news of Gen. Stone's arrest and confinement in Fort Lafayette. Why, was not known then, has never been known since; but as he still lives, to him the people must look for his vindication.

No wonder we were impatient to join in the movements that seemed to be closing in around the doomed traitors, as we called them. "They can't recover from this," we cried. Impatiently we waited. The 22d day of February, Abraham Lincoln, as Constitutional Commander of the Armies and Navies of the United States, appointed as the day for Gen. McClellan to move against the enemy. The President ordered it; and now, exulting in our prospects, we celebrated the birthday of Washington throughout the United States with joy, — we cheered for the victory that had followed victory; the hope that cheered us, we trusted, brought despair to our foe; the clouds were breaking away, and at last there was sunshine in our path; the dark path we had trodden for so many months at last emerging into glorious light. Proudly and buoyantly we tramped through Frederick to form in closed lines and listen to the reading of Washington's Farewell Address. And we were more than ever aroused to the conviction, that truly it was a great thing to live in this age and add one's might to this work.

Everything was hoped from Gen. McClellan, everything believed possible through him; and so sure did I, for one, feel in him and his conduct, that I sneered in derision at the anxiety of the politicians, heeded not the clamor about giving the country confidence or making the paper promises of the Government as valuable as gold.

On the 25th of February we were ordered to be in readiness to march, but the 27th came before we left our winter home. As we moved out for Frederick to take the cars for Harper's Ferry, again returning to that spot from whence so lately we had turned our backs, the men seemed almost wild with excitement; and as for me, with a full heart I exclaimed, "How sad and desolate were we in Virginia then, how sublime and triumphant now."

Printed in Dunstable, United Kingdom